FLOW JOURNAL

A DAILY GUIDE TO MASTER YOUR MINDSET

COLLIN HENDERSON

 @COLLINHENDERSON

 COLLIN HENDERSON

WWW.THECOLLINHENDERSON.COM

THIS JOURNAL BELONGS TO:

_____

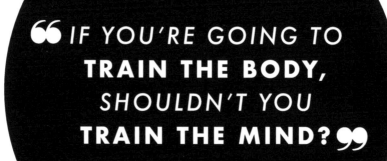

" *IF YOU'RE GOING TO* **TRAIN THE BODY,** *SHOULDN'T YOU* **TRAIN THE MIND? "**

- **RUSSELL WILSON**

INTRODUCTION

WHY SHOULD YOU JOURNAL?

I get it. Taking five to ten minutes out of your busy schedule to journal does not seem ideal. You have a lot going on, I'm sure. From managing your time, practice, competition, social life, work, or school...life is crazy. But that is the very reason why I'm encouraging you to make journaling a daily habit—to help you organize the chaos. Most performers spend hours on their physical and skill improvement but many do not carve out time to improve their mental fitness.

The *Flow Journal* was born from my years of study in the field of positive psychology, something I was drawn to because I struggled with stress and a lack of mental consistency for years. Being a starting two-sport athlete at the Division I level, I was too insecure to tell someone that I lacked confidence, was nervous, and didn't know how to handle my emotions. At the time, I felt like athletes should be tough and asking for help was a sign of weakness. Wow, was I completely wrong and misled. Being vulnerable is not a sign of weakness but a sign of strength—to be courageous enough to be your authentic self.

In my opinion, mental wellness is the number one element of sustained peak performance. With that in mind, I've researched not only what the top thought leaders in the field of high performance suggest, but I've also studied what high achievers do consistently. There are several key behaviors and patterns that these elite performers execute regularly.

I lacked these mental prompts and tools, which is why I've developed this system to help you unlock the most powerful force for any performer...and that is being in a state of flow.

WHAT IS FLOW?

The concept of "flow" was coined by positive psychologist Dr. Mihaly Csikszentmihalyi. This enlightened consciousness is where creativity and energy come flowing like water or a current of electricity. Flow is also called "being in the zone," where you feel challenged, energized, no sense of time, and performing without judgment. When you are in a flow state, you are fully present in the moment. In this peak state, your mindset is set to neutral thoughts—instead of judging negative or positive.

Take a moment and write down a time in your life when you were performing at your very best (when you were in the zone). When was it? What did you accomplish? What were your thoughts like? How did you feel?

_____

_____

_____

_____

_____

_____

_____

_____

Write down what habits and routines you were doing during that time and leading up to competition. Are you still executing those habits?

_____

_____

_____

_____

_____

_____

_____

THE POWER OF HABIT

There are three concepts I know to be true in dealing with high performance:

- **Winners do what others are not willing to do.** Are you fully committed or simply interested in being your absolute best?
- **Shape your habits, or your habits shape you.** Are you consistent with the daily actions needed to succeed?
- **You do not have to be sick to get better.** What are you doing to improve your performance even during times of success?

This mindfulness system will help you attack all three of those statements.

Question: How much time do you spend on social media, Netflix, or playing video games? There are 1,440 minutes in a day. Journaling just ten minutes is only 0.7% of your day. What if those ten minutes could make you 7% better? Would you do it? Competition is a game of inches, milliseconds, and often comes down to just one point on the scoreboard. Leave nothing to chance. Make performance journaling your secret weapon.

PURPOSE

Having a deep sense of purpose and meaning for your life is one of the most powerful performance enhancers there is. Before you take time to write down your goals, it's important to get clear on your *why* first. Below are a few questions to help you uncover your purpose.

Why do you play or compete?

_____

_____

_____

What motivates you? (circle one)

Fear   Accolades   Recognition   Being the Best

Why are you motivated by this (or something else)?

_____

_____

_____

Do you play to please someone else or do you play for the love of the competition?

_____

Why do you want success?

_____

_____

_____

_____

What feelings and emotions are you striving to experience?

_____

_____

_____

_____

The greats in any field have a deep drive, hunger, and desire to succeed. If your motivation comes from outside of your heart and spirit, it will be hard to sustain greatness. When you don't feel like working hard, or have urges to quit, go back to your *why* answers on the previous page. These emotions will help give you the grit to push through.

IDENTITY AND VALUES

Here are two thoughts on the power of knowing who you are and what you stand for:

- *With clear values decisions are easy.*
- *If you stand for nothing, you will fall for anything.*

Instead of fitting in, my hope is that you belong—most importantly with yourself first. You are your most important relationship. Take a moment and think about what emotions, feelings, actions, and states of being that are most important to you. These keywords can be described as your personal philosophy and values. Mentors, coaches, teachers, pastors, and people that have helped shape you can help inspire such guiding principles. To help you come up with your own guiding principles, use the prompts below.

Think of the most influential people in your life or who you look up to. Write down their name and what traits these individuals possess that you admire.

_____

_____

_____

_____

_____

_____

_____

When you are gone from this earth, what do you want other people to say about you and how you lived your life?

_____

_____

_____

_____

_____

_____

What is most important to your happiness?

_____

_____

_____

_____

What are the most important habits that have been instilled in you by your parents, coaches, and mentors?

_____

_____

_____

_____

_____

_____

PHILOSOPHY

Take a look at your answers on the previous page. Based on what you wrote down, take a moment and summarize, in twenty words or less, your personal philosophy on what is most important to you. This can be similar to a mission or vision statement.

_____

_____

_____

_____

_____

_____

_____

_____

_____

VALUES

Take a moment and circle eight keywords from your previous responses. Of those eight, select three to five words that have the most meaning to you. These will serve as your core values. Let these words guide your thoughts and behaviors to be the best version of you.

_____

_____

_____

_____

_____

"YOU DON'T NEED TO BE SICK TO GET BETTER "

- TREVOR MOAWAD

PROCESS

The definition of *process* is "mental and physical disciplines done consistently to aid performance." By developing a process, you will set yourself up to conserve more mental energy. Also, repetition is the mother of mastery. The more you perform an action both mentally and physically, the more you are creating stronger mental grooves that actually reshape your brain by a phenomenon called "neuroplasticity" in which you are literally changing your brain. The aim is to perform these quality movements and thoughts enough times that you create a state of unconscious competence where you can perform these actions without thinking. By predetermining and performing key actions consistently, you will help your brain get out of your body's way when it's time to perform.

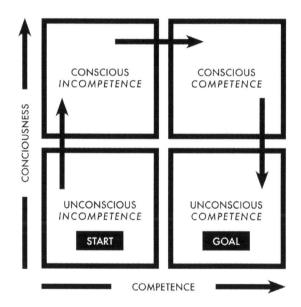

You only have so much mental energy in a day. Avoid decision fatigue by predetermining key habits, rituals, and routines that you will rely on during crunch time. Remember to focus on the process, not the pressure. Also, consistent routines provide a sense of comfort, which helps reduce stress during competitive situations.

TIP: Make these neural connections extra strong by consistently performing your routines and movements during the off-season and practice. When you start playing games and even during crucial moments, go back to these rituals and habits. This approach will help keep your concentration on executing key actions instead of worrying about what could go wrong.

List the actions and habits you commit to doing to help achieve greatness. Make sure you add a frequency or time you will complete each action.

_____

_____

_____

_____

_____

_____

_____

_____

_____

Actions: What are your top three most important commitments that will help you win (and when will you do them)?

-

-

-

PROCESS

Clothing and gear you will wear and use (equipment, shoes, socks, tape, under performance gear, etc.):

Pre-game music playlist or theme song:

Warm-up routine:

Pre-play routine:

Post-game routine:

When and where will I fill out my *Flow Journal?*

Pre (before competition):

Post (after competition):

Remember: We don't rise to the occasion, we rise to our training. Don't think you can just "turn it on" come game time. Develop and trust your process. The separation is in the preparation.

BALANCE

Sometimes as performers, we receive our validation and worthiness of love by how well we perform. This is a slippery slope. You are more than one thing. You are more than an athlete, musician, actor, or performer. To help you identify other parts of your life where you can feel validated and important, add to your *Me Wheel*. In the open spaces below, write in other areas of your life that make you who you are (other passions, activities, or things that are important to you. Examples: your faith, being a supportive friend, your scholastics, etc.). Revert to this diagram when you feel overly stressed due to the inner pressures of performance.

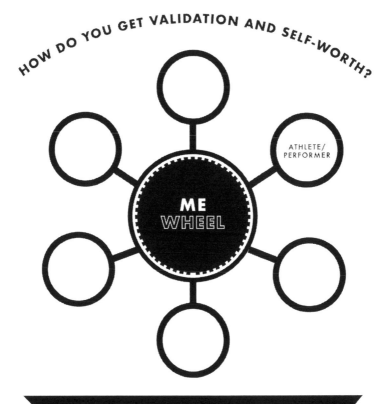

HOW DO YOU GET VALIDATION AND SELF-WORTH?

ATHLETE/
PERFORMER

ME
WHEEL

BE MORE THAN ONE THING.

RECOVERY

A key element to access flow is having a solid recovery plan. Proper sleep, hydration, and nutrition are factors that we can control. Research has shown that all three of these elements can improve reaction times, endurance, and focus. Leave nothing to chance. Gain a competitive advantage by taking ownership of your recovery. Remember: Nothing happens by accident!

Sleep plan:

Hours of sleep goal: _____

Time you will go to bed: _____

Time you will wake up: _____

Time you will take a nap: _____

Nutrition plan:

What bad foods do you crave that you will stay away from?

_____

_____

_____

What foods will you make essential to your diet?

_____

_____

_____

Hydration plan (water intake should be at least half of your body weight in ounces):

_____

_____

Meditation/visualization plan (where, when, and for how long will you meditate or visualize? Do you plan on using a guided mindfulness app like *Headspace*, *Calm*, or *Oak - Meditation and Breathing*?):

_____

_____

_____

_____

_____

_____

FOCUS ON THE ROOT NOT THE FRUIT

Sometimes as performers, our focus gets sidetracked by comparing and obtaining our validation on outcomes we cannot control. I call this being "seduced by the fruit"—focusing on stats and accolades, having an outcome-only focus, and obsessing over the opinions of others. This mental approach increases stress and hinders one's ability to play fully immersed in the moment. You can't control outcomes or what people think of you.

Instead, focus on what you can control, "the root"—your habits, commitments, and fundamentals. This type of focus is like the root of a tree—it is underground and cannot be seen. However, the root keeps the tree grounded and is vital for its survival. Similarly, your habits behind the scenes are often not recognized. But developing and trusting your process will lead to better production and consistency than receiving validation from the fruit.

FRUIT

WE CAN'T CONTROL:
OPINIONS, OUTCOMES, STATS, ACCOLADES, MEDIA

ROOT

WE CAN CONTROL:
HABITS, ROUTINES, PROCESS, VALUES, COMMITMENTS, TEAM-FIRST MINDSET

Fruit: List factors you cannot control that either distract you or are elements out of your control (for example: weather, officiating, social media, etc.).

_____

_____

_____

_____

Root: Write down commitments you will choose to focus on that you can control (for example: extra repetitions, hours of sleep, days in the weight room, etc.).

_____

_____

_____

_____

PRIME YOUR MINDSET

Repeated actions become instinct. If you use the *Flow Journal* as a part of your process, it can't hurt but only help you reach your goals and potential. One of the top performance psychologists in the world, Dr. Michael Gervais, says that journaling is an excellent way to gain clarity and wisdom from within. He also suggests that having a mindfulness practice is a precursor to flow. This system will help you be more mindful of your thoughts, experiences, and goals to help you quiet the noise and compete with a clear and peaceful mind.

Every performer does some sort of physical warm-up before competition. This mental performance system will help you warm-up your mindset, focus, and objectives for what you must do to be successful before and after you compete. Clarity is power.

Before you get started with daily journaling, let's cover what elements make up your *Flow Journal* and why they are included. Before competition, you will be prompted to fill out the **PRE section**. There are three main prompts that will help you focus on gratitude, affirmations, and your intention for that session, practice, or game. Later we will discuss the **POST section**, which you will fill out after practice or competition to help you gain self-awareness on your mindset during performance.

" *THE FIRST &* **GREATEST** **VICTORY** *IS OVER SELF.* **"**

— PLATO

PRE-FLOW

GRATITUDE

Having a consistent gratitude practice—in which you focus on things, people, and experiences that make you happy—is clinically proven to reduce the stress hormone cortisol. Gratitude has many other benefits such as lowering blood pressure, generating deeper relationships, and actually lengthening life. By making the act of thankfulness a foundation of your mindset, you will create an optimism that will help you deal with adversity and enjoy the journey. If you can learn to exchange expectation with appreciation, you will flat-out perform better.

Make a list (on the next page) of what you are grateful for. This list can include big things like people in your life and even small simple things like your favorite food or the feel of the breeze on your face. Reference this list daily—especially during times of adversity. Remember: It's impossible to be bitter, angry, worried, and grateful at the same time.

TIP: Create a gratitude ritual that you can implement before each practice or competition begins. Find a spot on the field or court and soak in the moment. Choose to feel gratitude for the opportunity to play and be alive.

Gratitude List:

_____

_____

_____

_____

_____

_____

_____

_____

_____

_____

_____

AFFIRMATIONS

How is your relationship with yourself? Words matter. According to Trevor Moawad, who is one of the top mental performance coaches in the country and works with University of Alabama Football and the Seattle Seahawks' Pro Bowl quarterback Russell Wilson: "What you say to yourself is ten times more powerful than what anyone can say to you." Quality thought = quality movement.

The reason why it is important to take control of your self-talk is because the human brain is designed to survive not thrive. The mind is naturally wired to protect your image, ego, and safety. This is not your true authentic self talking but your inner-judge. I believe there are two yous: *the Critic and the Creative.*

CRITIC VS. CREATIVE BRAIN

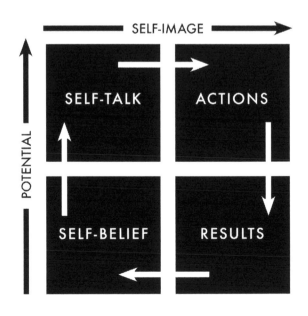

CRITIC	CREATIVE
PESSIMISTIC	OPTIMISTIC
COMPARES	CARES
INSECURE	CONFIDENT
VALIDATION IN OUTCOMES	VALIDATION IN EFFORT
AFRAID TO FAIL	SEES FAILURE AS GROWTH
OVER FOCUS OF SELF	UNSELFISH
PAST/FUTURE FOCUSED	IN THE NOW
CLOSE-MINDED	OPEN-MINDED

By writing down positive statements to yourself, you will be tapping into your creative brain, which will help improve your self-image. This positive mental shift sets a chain reaction to improve your actions and reach your potential.

SELF-IMAGE →

POTENTIAL

SELF-TALK	ACTIONS
SELF-BELIEF	RESULTS

To maximize the impact of affirmations, remember to support your affirming words with what actions you have done to solidify these positive internal statements…like the work you have put in or the results you have proven. By backing up your words with actions, you will build internal credibility with yourself, which will allow you to trust your preparation and generate confidence.

All-time Olympic champion swimmer Michael Phelps says that he gives himself an affirmation everytime he walks through a doorway. This habit helps improve his confidence to attack the day and competition. Prime your mindset like Phelps—use the *Flow Journal* to give yourself positive self-talk daily.

Take a moment and create a solid foundation of positive self-talk below.

What are your strengths?

_____

_____

_____

_____

What makes you unique from others?

_____

_____

_____

How can you turn a perceived weakness into a strength?

_____

_____

_____

_____

What accomplishments are you proud of?

_____

_____

_____

_____

What adversities, hardships, or failures have you overcome in your life?

_____

_____

_____

_____

_____

Use the above answers and responses to help take ownership of your self-talk and bounce back when you fail.

Below are internal phrases that have been proven to improve resilience, confidence, and performance. Remember to tell yourself these statements during challenging times.

- *I can do hard things.*
- *I'll do better next time.*

INTENTION

The best focus on less, not more. By setting a clear intention, you are helping your subconscious go after what your conscious brain wants. Research shows that performers who set a clear goal before practice and games are more likely to access a flow state. Performance psychologists sometimes call this "deliberate practice," in which you are very intentional with your movement, purpose, and accountability. Help your subconscious mind get locked-in. Begin each competition (practice with self or others and games) with a clear objective.

Describe what success looks like to you:

_____

_____

_____

_____

_____

How can you measure this?

_____

_____

_____

Write down your goals (look at this list consistently):

My personal goal for each competition:

_____

_____

My personal goal for the quarter (3 months):

_____

_____

My long-term (2-5 years) goal:

_____

_____

My goal for my team this season:

_____

_____

IMAGERY

Science has proven that your brain cannot tell the difference between physically performing an activity versus imagining doing that same event (using all of your senses). Neurons that fire together wire together. When you visualize, you are rehearsing actions that your subconscious brain can store and recall for later. Your brain says, "I've been here before. I know what to do." Visualizing helps you create neural pathways that help you stay in rhythm, move with more confidence, and create a clear path for your body to execute.

Once you have filled out the first half of your *Flow Journal*, take a moment to close your eyes, focus on your breath, and visualize what you wrote down using all of your senses (sight, sounds, touch, movement, smell, taste, etc.). I call this the HAW Method:
- I Have. (Gratitude)
- I Am. (Affirmations)
- I Will. (Intention)

Even if you do this exercise for just one to three minutes before competition, you will help prime your mindset to be more relaxed and focused on your objective.

When and where will you prioritize making mindfulness—quiet time to yourself where you focus on your breath and positive imagery—a priority for your performance?

_____

_____

_____

_____

_____

_____

**"I NEVER LOSE,
I EITHER WIN
OR I LEARN."**

- NELSON MANDELA

POST-FLOW

SELF-AWARENESS

Being clear on who you are, how you feel, and what you need to do is a competitive advantage. The POST section of the *Flow Journal* allows you to reflect on what you did well and evaluate what you need to do to improve.

The aim of this section is to help you assess your performance in several key areas. I call this the Three Truths. The goal for any workout or game is to answer "yes" to all three.

- *Was I present?* (Was I fully in the moment and not caught up in my past or future?)
- *Was I authentic?* (Did I perform as my true authentic self?)
- *Did I grow?* (Did I take necessary steps to improve?)

But before I break down the makeup of the POST section, it's important to uncover any mental or emotional roadblocks that are hindering your authenticity. Below are important questions to address to help stretch your comfort zone and not hide from shame and fear...but to attack it.

What is a common negative thought or mistake you replay in your mind that you feel holds you back from peak performance?

_____

_____

_____

_____

What causes my stress?

_____

_____

_____

I feel pressure from/when:

_____

_____

_____

Here are three steps to overcome these negative emotions and thought patterns:
1. Write it.
2. Read it.
3. Speak it.

Who is someone you trust that you can talk to about this?

_____

When will you talk to them?

_____

What positive actions can you take to address a fear that is holding you back?

_____

_____

_____

_____

Let shame, negative feelings, or mistakes live on this page rather than reoccurring in your brain.

GROWTH MINDSET

Ultimate fulfillment is found through learning and growing. This section of the *Flow Journal* is where you are invited to document what you learned from a specific day of competition. The goal is to foster what Stanford professor Dr. Carol Dweck calls a "growth mindset," one in which we are not defined by our mistakes but rather grow from success and failure. Do not waste a mistake. Write it down and use it to improve your game for next time. Perfection is the enemy of creativity. Push yourself to get comfortable being uncomfortable and not afraid to fail. Challenging your abilities and learning new skills helps trigger flow.

Instead of catastrophizing what can go wrong, what is a reset word and/or slogan you can say to yourself to help you respond to ANTs (Automatic Negative Thoughts) that pop up (especially after failure)? "I got this," "Breathe," or "Stay low" are possible examples of personal slogans to help snap one's mind back to the positive. This thought substitution technique will simplify your approach to one simple action.

Write your reset word and/or slogan here:

_____

_____

This reset word/slogan can also be called your "Power Statement." This mantra can be used when you feel nervous or have doubt. Kind of like how the timid Prince Adam transforms into the superhero He-Man and declares: "I have the power!"

Now list an image, object, or piece of equipment in the field or on the court that you can look at to refocus your mindset when you feel your heart rate rise.

_____

_____

Remember to take a deep breath and utilize controlled

35

breathing. Oxygen will give your body energy and lower your heart rate. Try to pay more attention to your inhale and exhale versus letting your mind play the "what-if" game. In moments of stress, put your hand on your stomach and feel your diaphragm rise and fall. With each breath, imagine you are inhaling courage and exhaling worry.

Peak performance does not live in the past or future, but in the now. Focus on the very next play...just one rep at a time. These techniques will help calm you down.

SERVICE

Throughout your journey of high performance, remember to think beyond just yourself and to serve your teammates. Research shows that true happiness is found in connection and relationships with others. Serving and helping others have been proven to release dopamine and serotonin, which are happy chemicals in the body. Believe it or not, working with others toward a common goal helps access flow. By being an unselfish and generous teammate, you will not only help others, but you will help yourself as well.

List how you like to be treated as a teammate. Share this with your team.

_____

_____

_____

What type of teammate do you strive to be? Make a list here.

_____

_____

_____

_____

_____

"WHAT YOU THINK YOU CREATE, *WHAT YOU FEEL* **YOU ATTRACT**, *WHAT YOU IMAGINE* **YOU BECOME."**

-UNKNOWN

LET'S GO!

The Greek philosopher Aristotle once said, "We are what we repeatedly do. Excellence, then, is not an act, but a habit." Just know that your greatest competition is not your opponent, but yourself. Take control of your mindset by utilizing this journal consistently. If you do, you will help your subconscious unlock the power of the flow.

To help you along your journey of self-betterment, I encourage you to have a *Flow Journal* accountability buddy (preferably a teammate) that you can share the answers above with and who can encourage you to stick to your process. Make sure it is someone you trust. No one should worry or win alone.

List that person's name here:

_____

Remember to fill the PRE section out before competition and the POST section after competition. You should treat this process the same when you practice by yourself, with others, during game time, and crunch time.

There are no big moments! Every repetition and moment is important—even practice. One play at a time. If you can put the same value in practice as you do for games, you will be less stressed and more focused come game time. Remember to always go back to your mental and physical routines. Focus on the process not the prize...the process not the pressure.

YOU GOT THIS!

The body has limits but the mind is limitless.

Win the inner-game, dominate the outer-game.

STRESS	ENERGY	RECOVERY
On a scale from 1-10 (1= low stress 10 = high stress) Circle One:	On a scale from 1-10 (1= low energy 10 = high energy) Circle One:	In the past 24 Hours
1 2 (3) 4 5 6 7 8 9 10	1 2 3 4 5 6 7 8 (9) 10	I slept for __9__ hours I napped for __15__ min. I practiced mindfulness for __6__ min.

HOW DO I FEEL TODAY?

I feel energized and rested. My night time discipline and routine of putting my phone away is really paying off. I've had 3 nights in a row of 9 hours of sleep.

GRATITUDE (I HAVE) — List recent small wins, things your experienced that made you happy, or what you are excited about.

I'm so pumped it's in the 70's all week - love working out in the sun. I can't wait to go on a date night tonight... So thankful for Amy.

AFFIRMATIONS (I AM) — Give yourself positive self-talk. What actions have supported these affirmations?

I'm deserving of being a champion. I've put in the work, and I'm seeing my effort pay off. I'm as worthy as anybody to be on this stage. Let's go!!!

INTENTION (I WILL) — What is one area of your performance that you will focus on and/or try to execute?

I'm going to be very intentional on keeping my hands back during batting practice. Recently I've been out in front on the ball, gotta keep my hands back!

BE PRESENT • BE AUTHENTIC • GROW DAILY
LET'S GO!!!

THOUGHTS	FOCUS	PROCESS
How was my self-talk today? Circle One:	How was my focus today? Add up to 100% :	Did I commit to my plan? **Y/N**
POSITIVE **NEUTRAL** NEGATIVE	**PAST: __%** **PRESENT: __%** **FUTURE: __%**	Did I seek feedback? **Y/N**

WHAT I DID WELL:

_____

_____

_____

WHAT I LEARNED:

_____

_____

_____

WHAT I WILL WORK ON TO IMPROVE:

_____

_____

_____

OTHER THOUGHTS:

_____

_____

_____

HOW CAN YOÚ BECOME WHAT YOU DON'T BELIEVE?

STRESS	**ENERGY**	**RECOVERY**
On a scale from 1-10	On a scale from 1-10	In the past 24 Hours
(1= low stress 10 = high stress)	(1= low energy 10 = high energy)	
Circle One:	Circle One:	I slept for _____ hours
1 2 3	1 2 3	I napped for _____ min.
4 5 6 7	**4 5 6 7**	I practiced mindfulness
8 9 10	**8 9 10**	for _____ min.

HOW DO I FEEL TODAY?

_____

_____

_____

GRATITUDE (I HAVE) — List recent small wins, things your experienced that made you happy, or what you are excited about.

_____

_____

_____

AFFIRMATIONS (I AM) — Give yourself positive self-talk. What actions have supported these affirmations?

_____

_____

_____

INTENTION (I WILL) — What is one area of your performance that you will focus on and/or try to execute?

_____

_____

BE PRESENT • BE AUTHENTIC • GROW DAILY

THOUGHTS	**FOCUS**	**PROCESS**
How was my self -talk today? Circle One:	How was my focus today? Add up to 100% :	Did I commit to my plan?
POSITIVE		**Y/N**
NEUTRAL	PAST: __%	
NEGATIVE	**PRESENT: __%**	Did I seek feedback?
	FUTURE: __%	**Y/N**

WHAT I DID WELL:

_____

_____

_____

WHAT I LEARNED:

_____

_____

_____

WHAT I WILL WORK ON TO IMPROVE:

_____

_____

_____

OTHER THOUGHTS:

_____

_____

_____

QUALITY THOUGHT = QUALITY MOVEMENT

STRESS	**ENERGY**	**RECOVERY**
On a scale from 1-10	On a scale from 1-10	In the past 24 Hours
(1= low stress 10 = high stress)	(1= low energy 10 = high energy)	I slept for _____ hours
Circle One:	Circle One:	I napped for _____ min.
1 2 3	1 2 3	I practiced mindfulness
4 5 6 7	**4 5 6 7**	for _____ min.
8 9 10	**8 9 10**	

HOW DO I FEEL TODAY?

_____

_____

_____

GRATITUDE (I HAVE) — List recent small wins, things your experienced that made you happy, or what you are excited about.

_____

_____

_____

AFFIRMATIONS (I AM) — Give yourself positive self-talk. What actions have supported these affirmations?

_____

_____

_____

INTENTION (I WILL) — What is one area of your performance that you will focus on and/or try to execute?

_____

_____

BE PRESENT · BE AUTHENTIC · GROW DAILY

THOUGHTS	FOCUS	PROCESS
How was my self -talk today? Circle One:	How was my focus today? Add up to 100% :	Did I commit to my plan?
POSITIVE		**Y/N**
NEUTRAL	**PAST: __%**	Did I seek feedback?
NEGATIVE	**PRESENT: __%**	**Y/N**
	FUTURE: __%	

WHAT I DID WELL:

_____

_____

_____

WHAT I LEARNED:

_____

_____

_____

WHAT I WILL WORK ON TO IMPROVE:

_____

_____

_____

OTHER THOUGHTS:

_____

_____

_____

JUST BE YOU

STRESS	**ENERGY**	**RECOVERY**
On a scale from 1-10	On a scale from 1-10	In the past 24 Hours
(1= low stress 10 = high stress)	(1= low energy 10 = high energy)	
Circle One:	Circle One:	I slept for _____ hours
1 2 3	1 2 3	I napped for _____ min.
4 5 6 7	**4 5 6 7**	I practiced mindfulness
8 9 10	**8 9 10**	for _____ min.

HOW DO I FEEL TODAY?

_____

_____

_____

GRATITUDE (I HAVE) — List recent small wins, things your experienced that made you happy, or what you are excited about.

_____

_____

_____

AFFIRMATIONS (I AM) — Give yourself positive self-talk. What actions have supported these affirmations?

_____

_____

_____

INTENTION (I WILL) — What is one area of your performance that you will focus on and/or try to execute?

_____

_____

BE PRESENT · BE AUTHENTIC · GROW DAILY

THOUGHTS	FOCUS	PROCESS
How was my self -talk today? Circle One:	How was my focus today? Add up to 100% :	Did I commit to my plan?
POSITIVE	PAST: __%	**Y/N**
NEUTRAL	**PRESENT: __%**	Did I seek feedback?
NEGATIVE	FUTURE: __%	**Y/N**

WHAT I DID WELL:

_____

_____

_____

WHAT I LEARNED:

_____

_____

_____

WHAT I WILL WORK ON TO IMPROVE:

_____

_____

_____

OTHER THOUGHTS:

_____

_____

_____

MORE ISN'T BETTER - BETTER IS BETTER

STRESS	**ENERGY**	**RECOVERY**
On a scale from 1-10	On a scale from 1-10	In the past 24 Hours
(1= low stress 10 = high stress)	(1= low energy 10 = high energy)	I slept for _____ hours
Circle One:	Circle One:	I napped for _____ min.
1 2 3	1 2 3	I practiced mindfulness
4 5 6 7	**4 5 6 7**	for _____ min.
8 9 10	**8 9 10**	

HOW DO I FEEL TODAY?

_____

_____

_____

GRATITUDE (I HAVE) — List recent small wins, things your experienced that made you happy, or what you are excited about.

_____

_____

_____

AFFIRMATIONS (I AM) — Give yourself positive self-talk. What actions have supported these affirmations?

_____

_____

_____

INTENTION (I WILL) — What is one area of your performance that you will focus on and/or try to execute?

_____

_____

BE PRESENT • BE AUTHENTIC • GROW DAILY

THOUGHTS	**FOCUS**	**PROCESS**
How was my self -talk today? Circle One:	How was my focus today? Add up to 100% :	Did I commit to my plan?
POSITIVE		**Y/N**
NEUTRAL	PAST: __%	
NEGATIVE	**PRESENT: __%**	Did I seek feedback?
	FUTURE: __%	**Y/N**

WHAT I DID WELL:

_____

_____

_____

WHAT I LEARNED:

_____

_____

_____

WHAT I WILL WORK ON TO IMPROVE:

_____

_____

_____

OTHER THOUGHTS:

_____

_____

_____

**WHAT YOU DO IN THE DARK
SHINES BRIGHT IN THE LIGHT**

STRESS	**ENERGY**	**RECOVERY**
On a scale from 1-10 (1= low stress 10 = high stress) Circle One:	On a scale from 1-10 (1= low energy 10 = high energy) Circle One:	In the past 24 Hours
1 2 3 **4 5 6 7** 8 9 10	1 2 3 **4 5 6 7** **8 9 10**	I slept for _____ hours I napped for _____ min. I practiced mindfulness for _____ min.

HOW DO I FEEL TODAY?

_____

_____

_____

GRATITUDE (I HAVE) — List recent small wins, things your experienced that made you happy, or what you are excited about.

_____

_____

_____

AFFIRMATIONS (I AM) — Give yourself positive self-talk. What actions have supported these affirmations?

_____

_____

_____

INTENTION (I WILL) — What is one area of your performance that you will focus on and/or try to execute?

_____

_____

BE PRESENT • BE AUTHENTIC • GROW DAILY

THOUGHTS	FOCUS	PROCESS
How was my self -talk today? Circle One:	How was my focus today? Add up to 100% :	Did I commit to my plan?
POSITIVE		**Y / N**
NEUTRAL	**PAST:** __%	Did I seek feedback?
NEGATIVE	**PRESENT: __%**	
	FUTURE: __%	**Y / N**

WHAT I DID WELL:

_____

_____

_____

WHAT I LEARNED:

_____

_____

_____

WHAT I WILL WORK ON TO IMPROVE:

_____

_____

_____

OTHER THOUGHTS:

_____

_____

_____

TRUST YOUR TRAINING

STRESS	**ENERGY**	**RECOVERY**
On a scale from 1-10	On a scale from 1-10	In the past 24 Hours
(1= low stress 10 = high stress)	(1= low energy 10 = high energy)	
Circle One:	Circle One:	I slept for _____ hours
1 2 3	1 2 3	I napped for _____ min.
4 5 6 7	**4 5 6 7**	I practiced mindfulness
8 9 10	**8 9 10**	for _____ min.

HOW DO I FEEL TODAY?

_____

_____

_____

GRATITUDE (I HAVE) — List recent small wins, things your experienced that made you happy, or what you are excited about.

_____

_____

_____

AFFIRMATIONS (I AM) — Give yourself positive self-talk. What actions have supported these affirmations?

_____

_____

_____

INTENTION (I WILL) — What is one area of your performance that you will focus on and/or try to execute?

_____

_____

BE PRESENT · BE AUTHENTIC · GROW DAILY

THOUGHTS	FOCUS	PROCESS
How was my self-talk today? Circle One:	How was my focus today? Add up to 100% :	Did I commit to my plan?
POSITIVE **NEUTRAL** **NEGATIVE**	**PAST:** ___% **PRESENT:** __% **FUTURE:** ___%	**Y/N** Did I seek feedback? **Y/N**

WHAT I DID WELL:

_____

_____

_____

WHAT I LEARNED:

_____

_____

_____

WHAT I WILL WORK ON TO IMPROVE:

_____

_____

_____

OTHER THOUGHTS:

_____

_____

_____

THE MOST IMPORTANT MOMENT IS ALWAYS NOW

STRESS	ENERGY	RECOVERY
On a scale from 1-10	On a scale from 1-10	In the past 24 Hours
(1= low stress 10 = high stress)	(1= low energy 10 = high energy)	
Circle One:	Circle One:	I slept for _____ hours
1 2 3	1 2 3	I napped for _____ min.
4 5 6 7	**4 5 6 7**	I practiced mindfulness
8 9 10	**8 9 10**	for _____ min.

HOW DO I FEEL TODAY?

_____

_____

_____

GRATITUDE (I HAVE) — List recent small wins, things your experienced that made you happy, or what you are excited about.

_____

_____

_____

AFFIRMATIONS (I AM) — Give yourself positive self-talk. What actions have supported these affirmations?

_____

_____

_____

INTENTION (I WILL) — What is one area of your performance that you will focus on and/or try to execute?

_____

_____

BE PRESENT • BE AUTHENTIC • GROW DAILY

THOUGHTS	**FOCUS**	**PROCESS**
How was my self-talk today? Circle One:	How was my focus today? Add up to 100% :	Did I commit to my plan?
POSITIVE	PAST: __%	**Y/N**
NEUTRAL	**PRESENT: __%**	Did I seek feedback?
NEGATIVE	FUTURE: __%	**Y/N**

WHAT I DID WELL:

WHAT I LEARNED:

WHAT I WILL WORK ON TO IMPROVE:

OTHER THOUGHTS:

FOCUS ON THE PROCESS NOT THE PRESSURE

STRESS	**ENERGY**	**RECOVERY**
On a scale from 1-10	On a scale from 1-10	In the past 24 Hours
(1= low stress 10 = high stress)	(1= low energy 10 = high energy)	I slept for _____ hours
Circle One:	Circle One:	I napped for _____ min.
1 2 3	1 2 3	I practiced mindfulness
4 5 6 7	**4 5 6 7**	for _____ min.
8 9 10	**8 9 10**	

HOW DO I FEEL TODAY?

_____

_____

_____

GRATITUDE (I HAVE) — List recent small wins, things your experienced that made you happy, or what you are excited about.

_____

_____

_____

AFFIRMATIONS (I AM) — Give yourself positive self-talk. What actions have supported these affirmations?

_____

_____

_____

INTENTION (I WILL) — What is one area of your performance that you will focus on and/or try to execute?

_____

_____

BE PRESENT · BE AUTHENTIC · GROW DAILY

THOUGHTS	FOCUS	PROCESS
How was my self-talk today? Circle One:	How was my focus today? Add up to 100% :	Did I commit to my plan? **Y/N**
POSITIVE **NEUTRAL** NEGATIVE	PAST: ___% **PRESENT: __%** FUTURE: __%	Did I seek feedback? **Y/N**

WHAT I DID WELL:

_____

_____

_____

WHAT I LEARNED:

_____

_____

_____

WHAT I WILL WORK ON TO IMPROVE:

_____

_____

_____

OTHER THOUGHTS:

_____

_____

_____

YOU ARE A BY-PRODUCT OF THE PEOPLE YOU HANG OUT WITH THE MOST...CHOOSE WISELY

STRESS	**ENERGY**	**RECOVERY**
On a scale from 1-10	On a scale from 1-10	In the past 24 Hours
(1= low stress 10 = high stress)	(1= low energy 10 = high energy)	
Circle One:	Circle One:	I slept for _____ hours
1 2 3	1 2 3	I napped for _____ min.
4 5 6 7	**4 5 6 7**	I practiced mindfulness
8 9 10	**8 9 10**	for _____ min.

HOW DO I FEEL TODAY?

_____

_____

_____

GRATITUDE (I HAVE) — List recent small wins, things your experienced that made you happy, or what you are excited about.

_____

_____

_____

AFFIRMATIONS (I AM) — Give yourself positive self-talk. What actions have supported these affirmations?

_____

_____

_____

INTENTION (I WILL) — What is one area of your performance that you will focus on and/or try to execute?

_____

_____

BE PRESENT • BE AUTHENTIC • GROW DAILY

THOUGHTS	FOCUS	PROCESS
How was my self-talk today? Circle One:	How was my focus today? Add up to 100% :	Did I commit to my plan?
POSITIVE	**PAST: __%**	**Y/N**
NEUTRAL	**PRESENT: __%**	Did I seek feedback?
NEGATIVE	**FUTURE: __%**	**Y/N**

WHAT I DID WELL:

_____

_____

_____

WHAT I LEARNED:

_____

_____

_____

WHAT I WILL WORK ON TO IMPROVE:

_____

_____

_____

OTHER THOUGHTS:

_____

_____

_____

RECOVERY IS JUST AS IMPORTANT AS GRINDING

PRE-FLOW

DATE:

STRESS	ENERGY	RECOVERY
On a scale from 1-10 (1= low stress 10 = high stress) Circle One:	On a scale from 1-10 (1= low energy 10 = high energy) Circle One:	In the past 24 Hours
1 2 3	1 2 3	I slept for _____ hours
4 5 6 7	**4 5 6 7**	I napped for _____ min.
8 9 10	**8 9 10**	I practiced mindfulness for _____ min.

HOW DO I FEEL TODAY?

_____

_____

_____

GRATITUDE (I HAVE) — List recent small wins, things your experienced that made you happy, or what you are excited about.

_____

_____

_____

AFFIRMATIONS (I AM) — Give yourself positive self-talk. What actions have supported these affirmations?

_____

_____

_____

INTENTION (I WILL) — What is one area of your performance that you will focus on and/or try to execute?

_____

_____

BE PRESENT • BE AUTHENTIC • GROW DAILY

POST-FLOW

THOUGHTS	FOCUS	PROCESS
How was my self-talk today? Circle One: POSITIVE **NEUTRAL** NEGATIVE	How was my focus today? Add up to 100% : PAST: __% **PRESENT: __%** FUTURE: __%	Did I commit to my plan? **Y/N** Did I seek feedback? **Y/N**

WHAT I DID WELL:

_____

_____

_____

WHAT I LEARNED:

_____

_____

_____

WHAT I WILL WORK ON TO IMPROVE:

_____

_____

_____

OTHER THOUGHTS:

_____

_____

_____

IF YOU DO WHAT YOU FEAR THE MOST, THERE'S NOTHING YOU CANNOT DO

STRESS	**ENERGY**	**RECOVERY**
On a scale from 1-10	On a scale from 1-10	In the past 24 Hours
(1= low stress 10 = high stress)	(1= low energy 10 = high energy)	
Circle One:	Circle One:	I slept for _____ hours
1 2 3	1 2 3	I napped for _____ min.
4 5 6 7	**4 5 6 7**	I practiced mindfulness
8 9 10	**8 9 10**	for _____ min.

HOW DO I FEEL TODAY?

_____

_____

_____

GRATITUDE (I HAVE) — List recent small wins, things your experienced that made you happy, or what you are excited about.

_____

_____

_____

AFFIRMATIONS (I AM) — Give yourself positive self-talk. What actions have supported these affirmations?

_____

_____

_____

INTENTION (I WILL) — What is one area of your performance that you will focus on and/or try to execute?

_____

_____

BE PRESENT • BE AUTHENTIC • GROW DAILY

THOUGHTS How was my self-talk today? Circle One: POSITIVE **NEUTRAL** NEGATIVE	**FOCUS** How was my focus today? Add up to 100% : PAST: __% **PRESENT: __%** FUTURE: __%	**PROCESS** Did I commit to my plan? **Y/N** Did I seek feedback? **Y/N**

WHAT I DID WELL:

_____
_____
_____

WHAT I LEARNED:

_____
_____
_____

WHAT I WILL WORK ON TO IMPROVE:

_____
_____
_____

OTHER THOUGHTS:

_____
_____
_____

TRUE COURAGE IS BEING VULNERABLE

STRESS	**ENERGY**	**RECOVERY**
On a scale from 1-10 (1= low stress 10 = high stress) Circle One:	On a scale from 1-10 (1= low energy 10 = high energy) Circle One:	In the past 24 Hours
1 2 3 **4 5 6 7** 8 9 10	1 2 3 **4 5 6 7** **8 9 10**	I slept for _____ hours I napped for _____ min. I practiced mindfulness for _____ min.

HOW DO I FEEL TODAY?

_____

_____

_____

GRATITUDE (I HAVE) — List recent small wins, things your experienced that made you happy, or what you are excited about.

_____

_____

_____

AFFIRMATIONS (I AM) — Give yourself positive self-talk. What actions have supported these affirmations?

_____

_____

_____

INTENTION (I WILL) — What is one area of your performance that you will focus on and/or try to execute?

_____

_____

BE PRESENT • BE AUTHENTIC • GROW DAILY

THOUGHTS	FOCUS	PROCESS
How was my self-talk today? Circle One:	How was my focus today? Add up to 100% :	Did I commit to my plan?
POSITIVE **NEUTRAL** **NEGATIVE**	**PAST: __%** **PRESENT: __%** **FUTURE: __%**	**Y/N** Did I seek feedback? **Y/N**

WHAT I DID WELL:

_____

_____

_____

WHAT I LEARNED:

_____

_____

_____

WHAT I WILL WORK ON TO IMPROVE:

_____

_____

_____

OTHER THOUGHTS:

_____

_____

_____

F.A.I.L. = FIRST ATTEMPT IN LEARNING

STRESS	**ENERGY**	**RECOVERY**
On a scale from 1-10	On a scale from 1-10	In the past 24 Hours
(1= low stress 10 = high stress)	(1= low energy 10 = high energy)	
Circle One:	Circle One:	I slept for _____ hours
1 2 3	1 2 3	I napped for _____ min.
4 5 6 7	**4 5 6 7**	I practiced mindfulness
8 9 10	**8 9 10**	for _____ min.

HOW DO I FEEL TODAY?

_____

_____

_____

GRATITUDE (I HAVE) — List recent small wins, things your experienced that made you happy, or what you are excited about.

_____

_____

_____

AFFIRMATIONS (I AM) — Give yourself positive self-talk. What actions have supported these affirmations?

_____

_____

_____

INTENTION (I WILL) — What is one area of your performance that you will focus on and/or try to execute?

_____

_____

BE PRESENT · BE AUTHENTIC · GROW DAILY

THOUGHTS	FOCUS	PROCESS
How was my self -talk today? Circle One:	How was my focus today? Add up to 100% :	Did I commit to my plan?
POSITIVE	**PAST: ___%**	**Y/N**
NEUTRAL	**PRESENT: __%**	Did I seek feedback?
NEGATIVE	**FUTURE: ___%**	**Y/N**

WHAT I DID WELL:

_____

_____

_____

WHAT I LEARNED:

_____

_____

_____

WHAT I WILL WORK ON TO IMPROVE:

_____

_____

_____

OTHER THOUGHTS:

_____

_____

_____

THE MOST POWERFUL FORCE
IS HOW YOU SEE YOURSELF

STRESS	**ENERGY**	**RECOVERY**
On a scale from 1-10 (1= low stress 10 = high stress) Circle One:	On a scale from 1-10 (1= low energy 10 = high energy) Circle One:	In the past 24 Hours
1 2 3	1 2 3	I slept for _____ hours
4 5 6 7	**4 5 6 7**	I napped for _____ min.
8 9 10	**8 9 10**	I practiced mindfulness for _____ min.

HOW DO I FEEL TODAY?

_____

_____

_____

GRATITUDE (I HAVE) — List recent small wins, things your experienced that made you happy, or what you are excited about.

_____

_____

_____

AFFIRMATIONS (I AM) — Give yourself positive self-talk. What actions have supported these affirmations?

_____

_____

_____

INTENTION (I WILL) — What is one area of your performance that you will focus on and/or try to execute?

_____

_____

BE PRESENT · BE AUTHENTIC · GROW DAILY

THOUGHTS	**FOCUS**	**PROCESS**
How was my self-talk today? Circle One:	How was my focus today? Add up to 100% :	Did I commit to my plan?
POSITIVE	PAST: __%	**Y/N**
NEUTRAL	**PRESENT: __%**	Did I seek feedback?
NEGATIVE	FUTURE: __%	**Y/N**

WHAT I DID WELL:

_____

_____

_____

WHAT I LEARNED:

_____

_____

_____

WHAT I WILL WORK ON TO IMPROVE:

_____

_____

_____

OTHER THOUGHTS:

_____

_____

_____

3 WAYS TO BE A "G"
GENEROSITY - GRACE - GRATITUDE

STRESS	ENERGY	RECOVERY
On a scale from 1-10	On a scale from 1-10	In the past 24 Hours
(1= low stress 10 = high stress)	(1= low energy 10 = high energy)	
Circle One:	Circle One:	I slept for _____ hours
1 2 3	1 2 3	I napped for _____ min.
4 5 6 7	**4 5 6 7**	I practiced mindfulness
8 9 10	**8 9 10**	for _____ min.

HOW DO I FEEL TODAY?

_____

_____

_____

GRATITUDE (I HAVE) — List recent small wins, things your experienced that made you happy, or what you are excited about.

_____

_____

_____

AFFIRMATIONS (I AM) — Give yourself positive self-talk. What actions have supported these affirmations?

_____

_____

_____

INTENTION (I WILL) — What is one area of your performance that you will focus on and/or try to execute?

_____

_____

BE PRESENT · BE AUTHENTIC · GROW DAILY

THOUGHTS	FOCUS	PROCESS
How was my self -talk today? Circle One:	How was my focus today? Add up to 100% :	Did I commit to my plan? **Y/N**
POSITIVE **NEUTRAL** NEGATIVE	PAST: __% **PRESENT: __%** FUTURE: __%	Did I seek feedback? **Y/N**

WHAT I DID WELL:

_____

_____

_____

WHAT I LEARNED:

_____

_____

_____

WHAT I WILL WORK ON TO IMPROVE:

_____

_____

_____

OTHER THOUGHTS:

_____

_____

_____

BE WHERE YOUR FEET ARE

STRESS	**ENERGY**	**RECOVERY**
On a scale from 1-10 (1= low stress 10 = high stress) Circle One:	On a scale from 1-10 (1= low energy 10 = high energy) Circle One:	In the past 24 Hours
1 2 3 **4 5 6 7** 8 9 10	1 2 3 **4 5 6 7** **8 9 10**	I slept for _____ hours I napped for _____ min. I practiced mindfulness for _____ min.

HOW DO I FEEL TODAY?

_____

_____

_____

GRATITUDE (I HAVE) — List recent small wins, things your experienced that made you happy, or what you are excited about.

_____

_____

_____

AFFIRMATIONS (I AM) — Give yourself positive self-talk. What actions have supported these affirmations?

_____

_____

_____

INTENTION (I WILL) — What is one area of your performance that you will focus on and/or try to execute?

_____

_____

BE PRESENT · BE AUTHENTIC · GROW DAILY

THOUGHTS	**FOCUS**	**PROCESS**
How was my self-talk today? Circle One:	How was my focus today? Add up to 100% :	Did I commit to my plan?
POSITIVE	PAST: ___%	**Y/N**
NEUTRAL	**PRESENT: __%**	Did I seek feedback?
NEGATIVE	FUTURE: ___%	**Y/N**

WHAT I DID WELL:

_____

_____

_____

WHAT I LEARNED:

_____

_____

_____

WHAT I WILL WORK ON TO IMPROVE:

_____

_____

_____

OTHER THOUGHTS:

_____

_____

_____

DO THINGS WITH PURPOSE, ON PURPOSE

STRESS	ENERGY	RECOVERY
On a scale from 1-10 (1= low stress 10 = high stress) Circle One:	On a scale from 1-10 (1= low energy 10 = high energy) Circle One:	In the past 24 Hours
1 2 3 **4 5 6 7** 8 9 10	1 2 3 **4 5 6 7** **8 9 10**	I slept for _____ hours I napped for _____ min. I practiced mindfulness for _____ min.

HOW DO I FEEL TODAY?

_____

_____

_____

GRATITUDE (I HAVE) — List recent small wins, things your experienced that made you happy, or what you are excited about.

_____

_____

_____

AFFIRMATIONS (I AM) — Give yourself positive self-talk. What actions have supported these affirmations?

_____

_____

_____

INTENTION (I WILL) — What is one area of your performance that you will focus on and/or try to execute?

_____

_____

BE PRESENT • BE AUTHENTIC • GROW DAILY

THOUGHTS	FOCUS	PROCESS
How was my self-talk today? Circle One:	How was my focus today? Add up to 100% :	Did I commit to my plan?
		Y/N
POSITIVE	PAST: ___%	Did I seek feedback?
NEUTRAL	**PRESENT: __%**	
NEGATIVE	FUTURE: ___%	**Y/N**

WHAT I DID WELL:

_____

_____

_____

WHAT I LEARNED:

_____

_____

_____

WHAT I WILL WORK ON TO IMPROVE:

_____

_____

_____

OTHER THOUGHTS:

_____

_____

_____

W.I.N. STANDS FOR:
WHAT'S IMPORTANT NOW

STRESS	**ENERGY**	**RECOVERY**
On a scale from 1-10	On a scale from 1-10	In the past 24 Hours
(1= low stress 10 = high stress)	(1= low energy 10 = high energy)	
Circle One:	Circle One:	I slept for _____ hours
1 2 3	1 2 3	I napped for _____ min.
4 5 6 7	**4 5 6 7**	I practiced mindfulness
8 9 10	**8 9 10**	for _____ min.

HOW DO I FEEL TODAY?

_____

_____

_____

GRATITUDE (I HAVE) — List recent small wins, things your experienced that made you happy, or what you are excited about.

_____

_____

_____

AFFIRMATIONS (I AM) — Give yourself positive self-talk. What actions have supported these affirmations?

_____

_____

_____

INTENTION (I WILL) — What is one area of your performance that you will focus on and/or try to execute?

_____

_____

BE PRESENT · BE AUTHENTIC · GROW DAILY

THOUGHTS	FOCUS	PROCESS
How was my self -talk today? Circle One:	How was my focus today? Add up to 100% :	Did I commit to my plan? **Y/N**
POSITIVE **NEUTRAL** NEGATIVE	PAST: __% **PRESENT: __%** FUTURE: __%	Did I seek feedback? **Y/N**

WHAT I DID WELL:

_____

_____

_____

WHAT I LEARNED:

_____

_____

_____

WHAT I WILL WORK ON TO IMPROVE:

_____

_____

_____

OTHER THOUGHTS:

_____

_____

_____

DOES THE ROOM LIGHT UP
WHEN YOU ENTER OR WHEN YOU LEAVE?

STRESS	**ENERGY**	**RECOVERY**
On a scale from 1-10	On a scale from 1-10	In the past 24 Hours
(1= low stress 10 = high stress)	(1= low energy 10 = high energy)	
Circle One:	Circle One:	I slept for _____ hours
1 2 3	1 2 3	I napped for _____ min.
4 5 6 7	**4 5 6 7**	I practiced mindfulness
8 9 10	**8 9 10**	for _____ min.

HOW DO I FEEL TODAY?

_____

_____

_____

GRATITUDE (I HAVE) — List recent small wins, things your experienced that made you happy, or what you are excited about.

_____

_____

_____

AFFIRMATIONS (I AM) — Give yourself positive self-talk. What actions have supported these affirmations?

_____

_____

_____

INTENTION (I WILL) — What is one area of your performance that you will focus on and/or try to execute?

_____

_____

BE PRESENT • BE AUTHENTIC • GROW DAILY

THOUGHTS	**FOCUS**	**PROCESS**
How was my self-talk today? Circle One:	How was my focus today? Add up to 100% :	Did I commit to my plan?
		Y/N
POSITIVE	**PAST: __%**	Did I seek feedback?
NEUTRAL	**PRESENT: __%**	**Y/N**
NEGATIVE	**FUTURE: __%**	

WHAT I DID WELL:

_____

_____

_____

WHAT I LEARNED:

_____

_____

_____

WHAT I WILL WORK ON TO IMPROVE:

_____

_____

_____

OTHER THOUGHTS:

_____

_____

_____

THOUGHTS INFLUENCE HOW WE FEEL.
HOW WE FEEL INFLUENCES HOW WE PERFORM.

STRESS	ENERGY	RECOVERY
On a scale from 1-10	On a scale from 1-10	In the past 24 Hours
(1= low stress 10 = high stress)	(1= low energy 10 = high energy)	
Circle One:	Circle One:	I slept for _____ hours
1 2 3	1 2 3	I napped for _____ min.
4 5 6 7	**4 5 6 7**	I practiced mindfulness
8 9 10	**8 9 10**	for _____ min.

HOW DO I FEEL TODAY?

_____

_____

_____

GRATITUDE (I HAVE) — List recent small wins, things your experienced that made you happy, or what you are excited about.

_____

_____

_____

AFFIRMATIONS (I AM) — Give yourself positive self-talk. What actions have supported these affirmations?

_____

_____

_____

INTENTION (I WILL) — What is one area of your performance that you will focus on and/or try to execute?

_____

_____

BE PRESENT • BE AUTHENTIC • GROW DAILY

THOUGHTS	FOCUS	PROCESS
How was my self -talk today? Circle One: POSITIVE **NEUTRAL** NEGATIVE	How was my focus today? Add up to 100% : PAST: __% **PRESENT: __%** FUTURE: __%	Did I commit to my plan? **Y/N** Did I seek feedback? **Y/N**

WHAT I DID WELL:

WHAT I LEARNED:

WHAT I WILL WORK ON TO IMPROVE:

OTHER THOUGHTS:

COURAGE COMES BEFORE CONFIDENCE

PRE-FLOW   DATE:

STRESS	ENERGY	RECOVERY
On a scale from 1-10 (1= low stress 10 = high stress) Circle One:	On a scale from 1-10 (1= low energy 10 = high energy) Circle One:	In the past 24 Hours
1 2 3	1 2 3	I slept for _____ hours
4 5 6 7	**4 5 6 7**	I napped for _____ min.
8 9 10	**8 9 10**	I practiced mindfulness for _____ min.

HOW DO I FEEL TODAY?

_____

_____

_____

GRATITUDE (I HAVE) — List recent small wins, things your experienced that made you happy, or what you are excited about.

_____

_____

_____

AFFIRMATIONS (I AM) — Give yourself positive self-talk. What actions have supported these affirmations?

_____

_____

_____

INTENTION (I WILL) — What is one area of your performance that you will focus on and/or try to execute?

_____

_____

BE PRESENT • BE AUTHENTIC • GROW DAILY

THOUGHTS	FOCUS	PROCESS
How was my self-talk today? Circle One:	How was my focus today? Add up to 100% :	Did I commit to my plan?
POSITIVE		**Y/N**
NEUTRAL	PAST: __%	Did I seek feedback?
NEGATIVE	**PRESENT: __%**	**Y/N**
	FUTURE: __%	

WHAT I DID WELL:

_____
_____
_____

WHAT I LEARNED:

_____
_____
_____

WHAT I WILL WORK ON TO IMPROVE:

_____
_____
_____

OTHER THOUGHTS:

_____
_____
_____

THERE ARE TWO PAINS IN LIFE: THE PAIN OF REGRET AND THE PAIN OF HARD WORK.

STRESS	**ENERGY**	**RECOVERY**
On a scale from 1-10	On a scale from 1-10	In the past 24 Hours
(1= low stress 10 = high stress)	(1= low energy 10 = high energy)	I slept for _____ hours
Circle One:	Circle One:	I napped for _____ min.
1 2 3	1 2 3	I practiced mindfulness
4 5 6 7	**4 5 6 7**	for _____ min.
8 9 10	**8 9 10**	

HOW DO I FEEL TODAY?

_____

_____

_____

GRATITUDE (I HAVE) — List recent small wins, things your experienced that made you happy, or what you are excited about.

_____

_____

_____

AFFIRMATIONS (I AM) — Give yourself positive self-talk. What actions have supported these affirmations?

_____

_____

_____

INTENTION (I WILL) — What is one area of your performance that you will focus on and/or try to execute?

_____

_____

BE PRESENT • BE AUTHENTIC • GROW DAILY

THOUGHTS

How was my
self -talk today?
Circle One:

POSITIVE
NEUTRAL
NEGATIVE

FOCUS

How was my focus today?
Add up to 100% :

PAST: ___%
PRESENT: __%
FUTURE: ___%

PROCESS

Did I commit to my plan?

Y/N

Did I seek feedback?

Y/N

WHAT I DID WELL:

WHAT I LEARNED:

WHAT I WILL WORK ON TO IMPROVE:

OTHER THOUGHTS:

FOCUS ON THE PROCESS NOT THE PRIZE

STRESS	**ENERGY**	**RECOVERY**
On a scale from 1-10	On a scale from 1-10	In the past 24 Hours
(1= low stress 10 = high stress)	(1= low energy 10 = high energy)	
Circle One:	Circle One:	I slept for _____ hours
1 2 3	1 2 3	I napped for _____ min.
4 5 6 7	**4 5 6 7**	I practiced mindfulness
8 9 10	**8 9 10**	for _____ min.

HOW DO I FEEL TODAY?

_____

_____

_____

GRATITUDE (I HAVE) — List recent small wins, things your experienced that made you happy, or what you are excited about.

_____

_____

_____

AFFIRMATIONS (I AM) — Give yourself positive self-talk. What actions have supported these affirmations?

_____

_____

_____

INTENTION (I WILL) — What is one area of your performance that you will focus on and/or try to execute?

_____

_____

BE PRESENT · BE AUTHENTIC · GROW DAILY

THOUGHTS	FOCUS	PROCESS
How was my self -talk today? Circle One:	How was my focus today? Add up to 100% :	Did I commit to my plan?
POSITIVE	PAST: __%	**Y/N**
NEUTRAL	**PRESENT: __%**	Did I seek feedback?
NEGATIVE	FUTURE: __%	**Y/N**

WHAT I DID WELL:

_____

_____

_____

WHAT I LEARNED:

_____

_____

_____

WHAT I WILL WORK ON TO IMPROVE:

_____

_____

_____

OTHER THOUGHTS:

_____

_____

_____

WORRYING IS BETTING AGAINST YOURSELF

PRE-FLOW

DATE:

STRESS	ENERGY	RECOVERY
On a scale from 1-10 (1= low stress 10 = high stress) Circle One: **1 2 3 4 5 6 7 8 9 10**	On a scale from 1-10 (1= low energy 10 = high energy) Circle One: **1 2 3 4 5 6 7 8 9 10**	In the past 24 Hours I slept for _____ hours I napped for _____ min. I practiced mindfulness for _____ min.

HOW DO I FEEL TODAY?

_____

_____

_____

GRATITUDE (I HAVE) — List recent small wins, things your experienced that made you happy, or what you are excited about.

_____

_____

_____

AFFIRMATIONS (I AM) — Give yourself positive self-talk. What actions have supported these affirmations?

_____

_____

_____

INTENTION (I WILL) — What is one area of your performance that you will focus on and/or try to execute?

_____

_____

BE PRESENT • BE AUTHENTIC • GROW DAILY

THOUGHTS

How was my
self -talk today?
Circle One:

POSITIVE
NEUTRAL
NEGATIVE

FOCUS

How was my focus today?
Add up to 100% :

PAST: __%
PRESENT: __%
FUTURE: __%

PROCESS

Did I commit to my plan?

Y/N

Did I seek feedback?

Y/N

WHAT I DID WELL:

_____

_____

_____

WHAT I LEARNED:

_____

_____

_____

WHAT I WILL WORK ON TO IMPROVE:

_____

_____

_____

OTHER THOUGHTS:

_____

_____

_____

WE RISE BY HELPING OTHERS

STRESS	ENERGY	RECOVERY
On a scale from 1-10	On a scale from 1-10	In the past 24 Hours
(1= low stress 10 = high stress)	(1= low energy 10 = high energy)	
Circle One:	Circle One:	I slept for _____ hours
1 2 3	1 2 3	I napped for _____ min.
4 5 6 7	**4 5 6 7**	I practiced mindfulness
8 9 10	**8 9 10**	for _____ min.

HOW DO I FEEL TODAY?

_____

_____

_____

GRATITUDE (I HAVE) — List recent small wins, things your experienced that made you happy, or what you are excited about.

_____

_____

_____

AFFIRMATIONS (I AM) — Give yourself positive self-talk. What actions have supported these affirmations?

_____

_____

_____

INTENTION (I WILL) — What is one area of your performance that you will focus on and/or try to execute?

_____

_____

BE PRESENT · BE AUTHENTIC · GROW DAILY

THOUGHTS	FOCUS	PROCESS
How was my self-talk today? Circle One:	How was my focus today? Add up to 100% :	Did I commit to my plan?
POSITIVE		**Y/N**
NEUTRAL	**PAST: __%**	Did I seek feedback?
NEGATIVE	**PRESENT: __%**	**Y/N**
	FUTURE: __%	

WHAT I DID WELL:

_____
_____
_____

WHAT I LEARNED:

_____
_____
_____

WHAT I WILL WORK ON TO IMPROVE:

_____
_____
_____

OTHER THOUGHTS:

_____
_____
_____

YOU WERE DESIGNED FOR A REASON

STRESS	**ENERGY**	**RECOVERY**
On a scale from 1-10 (1= low stress 10 = high stress) Circle One:	On a scale from 1-10 (1= low energy 10 = high energy) Circle One:	In the past 24 Hours
1 2 3	1 2 3	I slept for _____ hours
4 5 6 7	**4 5 6 7**	I napped for _____ min.
8 9 10	**8 9 10**	I practiced mindfulness for _____ min.

HOW DO I FEEL TODAY?

_____

_____

_____

GRATITUDE (I HAVE) — List recent small wins, things your experienced that made you happy, or what you are excited about.

_____

_____

_____

AFFIRMATIONS (I AM) — Give yourself positive self-talk. What actions have supported these affirmations?

_____

_____

_____

INTENTION (I WILL) — What is one area of your performance that you will focus on and/or try to execute?

_____

_____

BE PRESENT • BE AUTHENTIC • GROW DAILY

THOUGHTS	FOCUS	PROCESS
How was my self-talk today? Circle One: **POSITIVE NEUTRAL NEGATIVE**	How was my focus today? Add up to 100%: **PAST: __% PRESENT: __% FUTURE: __%**	Did I commit to my plan? **Y/N** Did I seek feedback? **Y/N**

WHAT I DID WELL:

_____
_____
_____

WHAT I LEARNED:

_____
_____
_____

WHAT I WILL WORK ON TO IMPROVE:

_____
_____
_____

OTHER THOUGHTS:

_____
_____
_____

CLUTCH MEANS DOING WHAT YOU NORMALLY CAN DO WHEN IT MATTERS MOST

DATE:

STRESS	ENERGY	RECOVERY
On a scale from 1-10	On a scale from 1-10	In the past 24 Hours
(1= low stress 10 = high stress)	(1= low energy 10 = high energy)	
Circle One:	Circle One:	I slept for _____ hours
1 2 3	1 2 3	I napped for _____ min.
4 5 6 7	**4 5 6 7**	I practiced mindfulness
8 9 10	**8 9 10**	for _____ min.

HOW DO I FEEL TODAY?

_____

_____

_____

GRATITUDE (I HAVE) — List recent small wins, things your experienced that made you happy, or what you are excited about.

_____

_____

_____

AFFIRMATIONS (I AM) — Give yourself positive self-talk. What actions have supported these affirmations?

_____

_____

_____

INTENTION (I WILL) — What is one area of your performance that you will focus on and/or try to execute?

_____

_____

BE PRESENT · BE AUTHENTIC · GROW DAILY

THOUGHTS

How was my
self -talk today?

Circle One:

POSITIVE

NEUTRAL

NEGATIVE

FOCUS

How was my focus today?
Add up to 100% :

PAST: __%

PRESENT: __%

FUTURE: __%

PROCESS

Did I commit to my plan?

Y/N

Did I seek feedback?

Y/N

WHAT I DID WELL:

_____
_____
_____

WHAT I LEARNED:

_____
_____
_____

WHAT I WILL WORK ON TO IMPROVE:

_____
_____
_____

OTHER THOUGHTS:

_____
_____
_____

**WE DON'T RISE TO THE OCCASION -
WE RISE TO OUR TRAINING**

STRESS	ENERGY	RECOVERY
On a scale from 1-10	On a scale from 1-10	In the past 24 Hours
(1= low stress 10 = high stress)	(1= low energy 10 = high energy)	I slept for _____ hours
Circle One:	Circle One:	I napped for _____ min.
1 2 3	1 2 3	I practiced mindfulness
4 5 6 7	**4 5 6 7**	for _____ min.
8 9 10	**8 9 10**	

HOW DO I FEEL TODAY?

_____

_____

_____

GRATITUDE (I HAVE) — List recent small wins, things your experienced that made you happy, or what you are excited about.

_____

_____

_____

AFFIRMATIONS (I AM) — Give yourself positive self-talk. What actions have supported these affirmations?

_____

_____

_____

INTENTION (I WILL) — What is one area of your performance that you will focus on and/or try to execute?

_____

_____

_____

BE PRESENT · BE AUTHENTIC · GROW DAILY

THOUGHTS	FOCUS	PROCESS
How was my self-talk today? Circle One:	How was my focus today? Add up to 100% :	Did I commit to my plan?
POSITIVE	PAST: ___%	**Y/N**
NEUTRAL	**PRESENT: __%**	Did I seek feedback?
NEGATIVE	FUTURE: __%	**Y/N**

WHAT I DID WELL:

_____

_____

_____

WHAT I LEARNED:

_____

_____

WHAT I WILL WORK ON TO IMPROVE:

_____

_____

_____

OTHER THOUGHTS:

_____

_____

_____

WHATEVER THE BRAIN CAN CONCEIVE AND BELIEVE, IT CAN ACHIEVE

STRESS	**ENERGY**	**RECOVERY**
On a scale from 1-10 (1= low stress 10 = high stress) Circle One:	On a scale from 1-10 (1= low energy 10 = high energy) Circle One:	In the past 24 Hours
1 2 3 **4 5 6 7** 8 9 10	1 2 3 **4 5 6 7** **8 9 10**	I slept for _____ hours I napped for _____ min. I practiced mindfulness for _____ min.

HOW DO I FEEL TODAY?

_____

_____

_____

GRATITUDE (I HAVE) — List recent small wins, things your experienced that made you happy, or what you are excited about.

_____

_____

_____

AFFIRMATIONS (I AM) — Give yourself positive self-talk. What actions have supported these affirmations?

_____

_____

_____

INTENTION (I WILL) — What is one area of your performance that you will focus on and/or try to execute?

_____

_____

BE PRESENT • BE AUTHENTIC • GROW DAILY

THOUGHTS	FOCUS	PROCESS
How was my self-talk today? Circle One:	How was my focus today? Add up to 100% :	Did I commit to my plan? **Y / N**
POSITIVE **NEUTRAL** NEGATIVE	PAST: ___% **PRESENT: __%** FUTURE: ___%	Did I seek feedback? **Y / N**

WHAT I DID WELL:

_____

_____

_____

WHAT I LEARNED:

_____

_____

_____

WHAT I WILL WORK ON TO IMPROVE:

_____

_____

_____

OTHER THOUGHTS:

_____

_____

_____

NO ONE SHOULD WIN OR WORRY ALONE

STRESS	**ENERGY**	**RECOVERY**
On a scale from 1-10	On a scale from 1-10	In the past 24 Hours
(1= low stress 10 = high stress)	(1= low energy 10 = high energy)	
Circle One:	Circle One:	I slept for _____ hours
1 2 3	1 2 3	I napped for _____ min.
4 5 6 7	**4 5 6 7**	I practiced mindfulness
8 9 10	**8 9 10**	for _____ min.

HOW DO I FEEL TODAY?

GRATITUDE (I HAVE) — List recent small wins, things your experienced that made you happy, or what you are excited about.

AFFIRMATIONS (I AM) — Give yourself positive self-talk. What actions have supported these affirmations?

INTENTION (I WILL) — What is one area of your performance that you will focus on and/or try to execute?

BE PRESENT · BE AUTHENTIC · GROW DAILY

THOUGHTS	FOCUS	PROCESS
How was my self-talk today? Circle One:	How was my focus today? Add up to 100% :	Did I commit to my plan?
POSITIVE	PAST: __%	**Y/N**
NEUTRAL	PRESENT: __%	Did I seek feedback?
NEGATIVE	FUTURE: __%	**Y/N**

WHAT I DID WELL:

_____

_____

_____

WHAT I LEARNED:

_____

_____

_____

WHAT I WILL WORK ON TO IMPROVE:

_____

_____

_____

OTHER THOUGHTS:

_____

_____

_____

GO THE EXTRA MILE - IT'S NEVER CROWDED

STRESS	**ENERGY**	**RECOVERY**
On a scale from 1-10	On a scale from 1-10	In the past 24 Hours
(1= low stress 10 = high stress)	(1= low energy 10 = high energy)	
Circle One:	Circle One:	I slept for _____ hours
1 2 3	1 2 3	I napped for _____ min.
4 5 6 7	**4 5 6 7**	I practiced mindfulness
8 9 10	**8 9 10**	for _____ min.

HOW DO I FEEL TODAY?

_____

_____

_____

GRATITUDE (I HAVE) — List recent small wins, things your experienced that made you happy, or what you are excited about.

_____

_____

_____

AFFIRMATIONS (I AM) — Give yourself positive self-talk. What actions have supported these affirmations?

_____

_____

_____

INTENTION (I WILL) — What is one area of your performance that you will focus on and/or try to execute?

_____

_____

_____

BE PRESENT · BE AUTHENTIC · GROW DAILY

THOUGHTS	FOCUS	PROCESS
How was my self -talk today? Circle One:	How was my focus today? Add up to 100% :	Did I commit to my plan?
POSITIVE		**Y/N**
NEUTRAL	PAST: __%	
NEGATIVE	**PRESENT: __%**	Did I seek feedback?
	FUTURE: __%	**Y/N**

WHAT I DID WELL:

_____

_____

_____

WHAT I LEARNED:

_____

_____

_____

WHAT I WILL WORK ON TO IMPROVE:

_____

_____

_____

OTHER THOUGHTS:

_____

_____

_____

ENERGY FLOWS WHERE FOCUS GOES

STRESS	**ENERGY**	**RECOVERY**
On a scale from 1-10	On a scale from 1-10	In the past 24 Hours
(1= low stress 10 = high stress)	(1= low energy 10 = high energy)	
Circle One:	Circle One:	I slept for _____ hours
1 2 3	1 2 3	I napped for _____ min.
4 5 6 7	**4 5 6 7**	I practiced mindfulness
8 9 10	**8 9 10**	for _____ min.

HOW DO I FEEL TODAY?

_____

_____

_____

GRATITUDE (I HAVE) — List recent small wins, things your experienced that made you happy, or what you are excited about.

_____

_____

_____

AFFIRMATIONS (I AM) — Give yourself positive self-talk. What actions have supported these affirmations?

_____

_____

_____

INTENTION (I WILL) — What is one area of your performance that you will focus on and/or try to execute?

_____

_____

BE PRESENT · BE AUTHENTIC · GROW DAILY

THOUGHTS	FOCUS	PROCESS
How was my self -talk today? Circle One: **POSITIVE NEUTRAL NEGATIVE**	How was my focus today? Add up to 100% : **PAST: __% PRESENT: __% FUTURE: __%**	Did I commit to my plan? **Y/N** Did I seek feedback? **Y/N**

WHAT I DID WELL:

_____

_____

_____

WHAT I LEARNED:

_____

_____

_____

WHAT I WILL WORK ON TO IMPROVE:

_____

_____

_____

OTHER THOUGHTS:

_____

_____

_____

HOW CAN YOU BECOME WHAT YOU DON'T BELIEVE?

STRESS	ENERGY	RECOVERY
On a scale from 1-10	On a scale from 1-10	In the past 24 Hours
(1= low stress 10 = high stress)	(1= low energy 10 = high energy)	
Circle One:	Circle One:	I slept for _____ hours
1 2 3	1 2 3	I napped for _____ min.
4 5 6 7	**4 5 6 7**	I practiced mindfulness
8 9 10	**8 9 10**	for _____ min.

HOW DO I FEEL TODAY?

_____

_____

_____

GRATITUDE (I HAVE) — List recent small wins, things your experienced that made you happy, or what you are excited about.

_____

_____

_____

AFFIRMATIONS (I AM) — Give yourself positive self-talk. What actions have supported these affirmations?

_____

_____

_____

INTENTION (I WILL) — What is one area of your performance that you will focus on and/or try to execute?

_____

_____

BE PRESENT · BE AUTHENTIC · GROW DAILY

POST-FLOW

THOUGHTS	FOCUS	PROCESS
How was my self-talk today? Circle One:	How was my focus today? Add up to 100% :	Did I commit to my plan?
POSITIVE	PAST: __%	**Y/N**
NEUTRAL	**PRESENT: __%**	Did I seek feedback?
NEGATIVE	FUTURE: __%	**Y/N**

WHAT I DID WELL:

_____
_____
_____

WHAT I LEARNED:

_____
_____
_____

WHAT I WILL WORK ON TO IMPROVE:

_____
_____
_____

OTHER THOUGHTS:

_____
_____
_____

QUALITY THOUGHT = QUALITY MOVEMENT

PRE-FLOW

DATE:

STRESS	ENERGY	RECOVERY
On a scale from 1-10 (1= low stress 10 = high stress) Circle One:	On a scale from 1-10 (1= low energy 10 = high energy) Circle One:	In the past 24 Hours
1 2 3 **4 5 6 7** 8 9 10	1 2 3 **4 5 6 7** **8 9 10**	I slept for _____ hours I napped for _____ min. I practiced mindfulness for _____ min.

HOW DO I FEEL TODAY?

_____

_____

_____

GRATITUDE (I HAVE) — List recent small wins, things your experienced that made you happy, or what you are excited about.

_____

_____

_____

AFFIRMATIONS (I AM) — Give yourself positive self-talk. What actions have supported these affirmations?

_____

_____

_____

INTENTION (I WILL) — What is one area of your performance that you will focus on and/or try to execute?

_____

_____

BE PRESENT · BE AUTHENTIC · GROW DAILY

THOUGHTS
How was my self-talk today?
Circle One:
POSITIVE
NEUTRAL
NEGATIVE

FOCUS
How was my focus today?
Add up to 100% :
PAST: ___%
PRESENT: __%
FUTURE: ___%

PROCESS
Did I commit to my plan?
Y/N
Did I seek feedback?
Y/N

WHAT I DID WELL:

WHAT I LEARNED:

WHAT I WILL WORK ON TO IMPROVE:

OTHER THOUGHTS:

JUST BE YOU

STRESS	ENERGY	RECOVERY
On a scale from 1-10 (1= low stress 10 = high stress) Circle One:	On a scale from 1-10 (1= low energy 10 = high energy) Circle One:	In the past 24 Hours
1 2 3 **4 5 6 7** 8 9 10	1 2 3 **4 5 6 7** **8 9 10**	I slept for _____ hours I napped for _____ min. I practiced mindfulness for _____ min.

HOW DO I FEEL TODAY?

_____

_____

_____

GRATITUDE (I HAVE) — List recent small wins, things your experienced that made you happy, or what you are excited about.

_____

_____

_____

AFFIRMATIONS (I AM) — Give yourself positive self-talk. What actions have supported these affirmations?

_____

_____

_____

INTENTION (I WILL) — What is one area of your performance that you will focus on and/or try to execute?

_____

_____

BE PRESENT • BE AUTHENTIC • GROW DAILY

THOUGHTS
How was my
self -talk today?
Circle One:

POSITIVE
NEUTRAL
NEGATIVE

FOCUS
How was my focus today?
Add up to 100% :

PAST: ___%
PRESENT: __%
FUTURE: ___%

PROCESS
Did I commit to my plan?
Y/N
Did I seek feedback?
Y/N

WHAT I DID WELL:

_____
_____
_____

WHAT I LEARNED:

_____
_____
_____

WHAT I WILL WORK ON TO IMPROVE:

_____
_____
_____

OTHER THOUGHTS:

_____
_____
_____

MORE ISN'T BETTER - BETTER IS BETTER

STRESS	**ENERGY**	**RECOVERY**
On a scale from 1-10	On a scale from 1-10	In the past 24 Hours
(1= low stress 10 = high stress)	(1= low energy 10 = high energy)	
Circle One:	Circle One:	I slept for _____ hours
1 2 3	1 2 3	I napped for _____ min.
4 5 6 7	**4 5 6 7**	I practiced mindfulness
8 9 10	**8 9 10**	for _____ min.

HOW DO I FEEL TODAY?

_____

_____

_____

GRATITUDE (I HAVE) — List recent small wins, things your experienced that made you happy, or what you are excited about.

_____

_____

_____

AFFIRMATIONS (I AM) — Give yourself positive self-talk. What actions have supported these affirmations?

_____

_____

_____

INTENTION (I WILL) — What is one area of your performance that you will focus on and/or try to execute?

_____

_____

BE PRESENT • BE AUTHENTIC • GROW DAILY

THOUGHTS	**FOCUS**	**PROCESS**
How was my self-talk today? Circle One:	How was my focus today? Add up to 100% :	Did I commit to my plan?
POSITIVE	PAST: __%	**Y / N**
NEUTRAL	**PRESENT: __%**	Did I seek feedback?
NEGATIVE	FUTURE: __%	**Y / N**

WHAT I DID WELL:

_____
_____
_____

WHAT I LEARNED:

_____
_____
_____

WHAT I WILL WORK ON TO IMPROVE:

_____
_____
_____

OTHER THOUGHTS:

_____
_____
_____

**WHAT YOU DO IN THE DARK
SHINES BRIGHT IN THE LIGHT**

STRESS	ENERGY	RECOVERY
On a scale from 1-10 (1= low stress 10 = high stress) Circle One:	On a scale from 1-10 (1= low energy 10 = high energy) Circle One:	In the past 24 Hours
1 2 3 **4 5 6 7** 8 9 10	1 2 3 **4 5 6 7** **8 9 10**	I slept for _____ hours I napped for _____ min. I practiced mindfulness for _____ min.

HOW DO I FEEL TODAY?

_____

_____

_____

GRATITUDE (I HAVE) — List recent small wins, things your experienced that made you happy, or what you are excited about.

_____

_____

_____

AFFIRMATIONS (I AM) — Give yourself positive self-talk. What actions have supported these affirmations?

_____

_____

_____

INTENTION (I WILL) — What is one area of your performance that you will focus on and/or try to execute?

_____

_____

BE PRESENT • BE AUTHENTIC • GROW DAILY

THOUGHTS	FOCUS	PROCESS
How was my self-talk today? Circle One:	How was my focus today? Add up to 100% :	Did I commit to my plan? Y/N
POSITIVE NEUTRAL NEGATIVE	PAST: __% PRESENT: __% FUTURE: __%	Did I seek feedback? Y/N

WHAT I DID WELL:

_____
_____
_____

WHAT I LEARNED:

_____
_____
_____

WHAT I WILL WORK ON TO IMPROVE:

_____
_____
_____

OTHER THOUGHTS:

_____
_____
_____

TRUST YOUR TRAINING

STRESS	ENERGY	RECOVERY
On a scale from 1-10 (1= low stress 10 = high stress) Circle One:	On a scale from 1-10 (1= low energy 10 = high energy) Circle One:	In the past 24 Hours
1 2 3 **4 5 6 7** 8 9 10	1 2 3 **4 5 6 7** **8 9 10**	I slept for _____ hours I napped for _____ min. I practiced mindfulness for _____ min.

HOW DO I FEEL TODAY?

_____

_____

_____

GRATITUDE (I HAVE) — List recent small wins, things your experienced that made you happy, or what you are excited about.

_____

_____

_____

AFFIRMATIONS (I AM) — Give yourself positive self-talk. What actions have supported these affirmations?

_____

_____

_____

INTENTION (I WILL) — What is one area of your performance that you will focus on and/or try to execute?

_____

_____

BE PRESENT · BE AUTHENTIC · GROW DAILY

THOUGHTS	FOCUS	PROCESS
How was my self -talk today? Circle One:	How was my focus today? Add up to 100% :	Did I commit to my plan?
POSITIVE	PAST: __%	**Y/N**
NEUTRAL	**PRESENT: __%**	Did I seek feedback?
NEGATIVE	FUTURE: __%	**Y/N**

WHAT I DID WELL:

_____

_____

_____

WHAT I LEARNED:

_____

_____

_____

WHAT I WILL WORK ON TO IMPROVE:

_____

_____

_____

OTHER THOUGHTS:

_____

_____

_____

THE MOST IMPORTANT MOMENT IS ALWAYS NOW

STRESS	ENERGY	RECOVERY
On a scale from 1-10	On a scale from 1-10	In the past 24 Hours
(1= low stress 10 = high stress)	(1= low energy 10 = high energy)	
Circle One:	Circle One:	I slept for _____ hours
1 2 3	1 2 3	I napped for _____ min.
4 5 6 7	**4 5 6 7**	I practiced mindfulness
8 9 10	**8 9 10**	for _____ min.

HOW DO I FEEL TODAY?

_____

_____

_____

GRATITUDE (I HAVE) — List recent small wins, things your experienced that made you happy, or what you are excited about.

_____

_____

_____

AFFIRMATIONS (I AM) — Give yourself positive self-talk. What actions have supported these affirmations?

_____

_____

_____

INTENTION (I WILL) — What is one area of your performance that you will focus on and/or try to execute?

_____

_____

BE PRESENT · BE AUTHENTIC · GROW DAILY

THOUGHTS	FOCUS	PROCESS
How was my self-talk today? Circle One:	How was my focus today? Add up to 100% :	Did I commit to my plan?
POSITIVE		**Y/N**
NEUTRAL	PAST: ___%	Did I seek feedback?
NEGATIVE	**PRESENT: __%**	**Y/N**
	FUTURE: ___%	

WHAT I DID WELL:

_____
_____
_____

WHAT I LEARNED:

_____
_____
_____

WHAT I WILL WORK ON TO IMPROVE:

_____
_____
_____

OTHER THOUGHTS:

_____
_____
_____

FOCUS ON THE PROCESS NOT THE PRESSURE

STRESS	ENERGY	RECOVERY
On a scale from 1-10 (1= low stress 10 = high stress) Circle One:	On a scale from 1-10 (1= low energy 10 = high energy) Circle One:	In the past 24 Hours
1 2 3	1 2 3	I slept for _____ hours
4 5 6 7	**4 5 6 7**	I napped for _____ min.
8 9 10	**8 9 10**	I practiced mindfulness for _____ min.

HOW DO I FEEL TODAY?

_____

_____

_____

GRATITUDE (I HAVE) — List recent small wins, things your experienced that made you happy, or what you are excited about.

_____

_____

_____

AFFIRMATIONS (I AM) — Give yourself positive self-talk. What actions have supported these affirmations?

_____

_____

_____

INTENTION (I WILL) — What is one area of your performance that you will focus on and/or try to execute?

_____

_____

_____

BE PRESENT • BE AUTHENTIC • GROW DAILY

THOUGHTS	**FOCUS**	**PROCESS**
How was my self -talk today? Circle One:	How was my focus today? Add up to 100% :	Did I commit to my plan?
POSITIVE	PAST: __%	**Y/N**
NEUTRAL	**PRESENT: __%**	Did I seek feedback?
NEGATIVE	FUTURE: __%	**Y/N**

WHAT I DID WELL:

_____

_____

_____

WHAT I LEARNED:

_____

_____

_____

WHAT I WILL WORK ON TO IMPROVE:

_____

_____

_____

OTHER THOUGHTS:

_____

_____

_____

YOU ARE A BY-PRODUCT OF THE PEOPLE YOU HANG OUT WITH THE MOST...CHOOSE WISELY

STRESS	**ENERGY**	**RECOVERY**
On a scale from 1-10 (1= low stress 10 = high stress) Circle One:	On a scale from 1-10 (1= low energy 10 = high energy) Circle One:	In the past 24 Hours
1 2 3	1 2 3	I slept for _____ hours
4 5 6 7	**4 5 6 7**	I napped for _____ min.
8 9 10	**8 9 10**	I practiced mindfulness for _____ min.

HOW DO I FEEL TODAY?

_____

_____

_____

GRATITUDE (I HAVE) — List recent small wins, things your experienced that made you happy, or what you are excited about.

_____

_____

_____

AFFIRMATIONS (I AM) — Give yourself positive self-talk. What actions have supported these affirmations?

_____

_____

_____

INTENTION (I WILL) — What is one area of your performance that you will focus on and/or try to execute?

_____

_____

BE PRESENT · BE AUTHENTIC · GROW DAILY

THOUGHTS	FOCUS	PROCESS
How was my self-talk today? Circle One:	How was my focus today? Add up to 100% :	Did I commit to my plan? **Y/N**
POSITIVE **NEUTRAL** NEGATIVE	PAST: __% **PRESENT: __%** FUTURE: __%	Did I seek feedback? **Y/N**

WHAT I DID WELL:

_____
_____
_____

WHAT I LEARNED:

_____
_____
_____

WHAT I WILL WORK ON TO IMPROVE:

_____
_____
_____

OTHER THOUGHTS:

_____
_____
_____

RECOVERY IS JUST AS IMPORTANT AS GRINDING

STRESS	**ENERGY**	**RECOVERY**
On a scale from 1-10	On a scale from 1-10	In the past 24 Hours
(1= low stress 10 = high stress)	(1= low energy 10 = high energy)	I slept for _____ hours
Circle One:	Circle One:	I napped for _____ min.
1 2 3	1 2 3	I practiced mindfulness
4 5 6 7	**4 5 6 7**	for _____ min.
8 9 10	**8 9 10**	

HOW DO I FEEL TODAY?

_____

_____

_____

GRATITUDE (I HAVE) — List recent small wins, things your experienced that made you happy, or what you are excited about.

_____

_____

_____

AFFIRMATIONS (I AM) — Give yourself positive self-talk. What actions have supported these affirmations?

_____

_____

_____

INTENTION (I WILL) — What is one area of your performance that you will focus on and/or try to execute?

_____

_____

BE PRESENT · BE AUTHENTIC · GROW DAILY

THOUGHTS	FOCUS	PROCESS
How was my self-talk today? Circle One:	How was my focus today? Add up to 100% :	Did I commit to my plan?
POSITIVE		**Y/N**
NEUTRAL	PAST: __%	Did I seek feedback?
NEGATIVE	**PRESENT: __%**	**Y/N**
	FUTURE: __%	

WHAT I DID WELL:

_____

_____

_____

WHAT I LEARNED:

_____

_____

_____

WHAT I WILL WORK ON TO IMPROVE:

_____

_____

_____

OTHER THOUGHTS:

_____

_____

_____

IF YOU DO WHAT YOU FEAR THE MOST, THERE'S NOTHING YOU CANNOT DO

STRESS	**ENERGY**	**RECOVERY**
On a scale from 1-10 (1= low stress 10 = high stress) Circle One:	On a scale from 1-10 (1= low energy 10 = high energy) Circle One:	In the past 24 Hours
1 2 3	1 2 3	I slept for _____ hours
4 5 6 7	**4 5 6 7**	I napped for _____ min.
8 9 10	**8 9 10**	I practiced mindfulness for _____ min.

HOW DO I FEEL TODAY?

_____

_____

_____

GRATITUDE (I HAVE) — List recent small wins, things your experienced that made you happy, or what you are excited about.

_____

_____

_____

AFFIRMATIONS (I AM) — Give yourself positive self-talk. What actions have supported these affirmations?

_____

_____

_____

INTENTION (I WILL) — What is one area of your performance that you will focus on and/or try to execute?

_____

_____

BE PRESENT · BE AUTHENTIC · GROW DAILY

THOUGHTS	FOCUS	PROCESS
How was my self -talk today? Circle One:	How was my focus today? Add up to 100% :	Did I commit to my plan?
POSITIVE **NEUTRAL** **NEGATIVE**	**PAST: __%** **PRESENT: __%** **FUTURE: __%**	**Y/N** Did I seek feedback? **Y/N**

WHAT I DID WELL:

_____

_____

_____

WHAT I LEARNED:

_____

_____

_____

WHAT I WILL WORK ON TO IMPROVE:

_____

_____

_____

OTHER THOUGHTS:

_____

_____

_____

TRUE COURAGE IS BEING VULNERABLE

STRESS	**ENERGY**	**RECOVERY**
On a scale from 1-10	On a scale from 1-10	In the past 24 Hours
(1= low stress 10 = high stress)	(1= low energy 10 = high energy)	
Circle One:	Circle One:	I slept for _____ hours
1 2 3	1 2 3	I napped for _____ min.
4 5 6 7	**4 5 6 7**	I practiced mindfulness
8 9 10	**8 9 10**	for _____ min.

HOW DO I FEEL TODAY?

_____

_____

_____

GRATITUDE (I HAVE) — List recent small wins, things your experienced that made you happy, or what you are excited about.

_____

_____

_____

AFFIRMATIONS (I AM) — Give yourself positive self-talk. What actions have supported these affirmations?

_____

_____

_____

INTENTION (I WILL) — What is one area of your performance that you will focus on and/or try to execute?

_____

_____

BE PRESENT • BE AUTHENTIC • GROW DAILY

THOUGHTS	**FOCUS**	**PROCESS**
How was my self-talk today? Circle One: **POSITIVE NEUTRAL NEGATIVE**	How was my focus today? Add up to 100% : **PAST: __% PRESENT: __% FUTURE: __%**	Did I commit to my plan? **Y/N** Did I seek feedback? **Y/N**

WHAT I DID WELL:

_____

_____

_____

WHAT I LEARNED:

_____

_____

_____

WHAT I WILL WORK ON TO IMPROVE:

_____

_____

_____

OTHER THOUGHTS:

_____

_____

_____

F.A.I.L. = FIRST ATTEMPT IN LEARNING

STRESS	**ENERGY**	**RECOVERY**
On a scale from 1-10 (1= low stress 10 = high stress) Circle One:	On a scale from 1-10 (1= low energy 10 = high energy) Circle One:	In the past 24 Hours
1 2 3	1 2 3	I slept for _____ hours
4 5 6 7	**4 5 6 7**	I napped for _____ min.
8 9 10	**8 9 10**	I practiced mindfulness for _____ min.

HOW DO I FEEL TODAY?

_____

_____

_____

GRATITUDE (I HAVE) — List recent small wins, things your experienced that made you happy, or what you are excited about.

_____

_____

_____

AFFIRMATIONS (I AM) — Give yourself positive self-talk. What actions have supported these affirmations?

_____

_____

_____

INTENTION (I WILL) — What is one area of your performance that you will focus on and/or try to execute?

_____

_____

BE PRESENT • BE AUTHENTIC • GROW DAILY

THOUGHTS
How was my self-talk today?
Circle One:

POSITIVE
NEUTRAL
NEGATIVE

FOCUS
How was my focus today?
Add up to 100%:

PAST: ___%
PRESENT: __%
FUTURE: __%

PROCESS
Did I commit to my plan?

Y/N

Did I seek feedback?

Y/N

WHAT I DID WELL:

_____
_____
_____

WHAT I LEARNED:

_____
_____
_____

WHAT I WILL WORK ON TO IMPROVE:

_____
_____
_____

OTHER THOUGHTS:

_____
_____
_____

**THE MOST POWERFUL FORCE
IS HOW YOU SEE YOURSELF**

STRESS	**ENERGY**	**RECOVERY**
On a scale from 1-10	On a scale from 1-10	In the past 24 Hours
(1= low stress 10 = high stress)	(1= low energy 10 = high energy)	I slept for _____ hours
Circle One:	Circle One:	I napped for _____ min.
1 2 3	1 2 3	I practiced mindfulness
4 5 6 7	**4 5 6 7**	for _____ min.
8 9 10	**8 9 10**	

HOW DO I FEEL TODAY?

_____

_____

_____

GRATITUDE (I HAVE) — List recent small wins, things your experienced that made you happy, or what you are excited about.

_____

_____

_____

AFFIRMATIONS (I AM) — Give yourself positive self-talk. What actions have supported these affirmations?

_____

_____

_____

INTENTION (I WILL) — What is one area of your performance that you will focus on and/or try to execute?

_____

_____

BE PRESENT • BE AUTHENTIC • GROW DAILY

THOUGHTS	FOCUS	PROCESS
How was my self -talk today? Circle One:	How was my focus today? Add up to 100% :	Did I commit to my plan?
POSITIVE		**Y/N**
NEUTRAL	PAST: __%	
NEGATIVE	**PRESENT: __%**	Did I seek feedback?
	FUTURE: __%	**Y/N**

WHAT I DID WELL:

_____

_____

_____

WHAT I LEARNED:

_____

_____

_____

WHAT I WILL WORK ON TO IMPROVE:

_____

_____

_____

OTHER THOUGHTS:

_____

_____

_____

3 WAYS TO BE A "G"
GENEROSITY - GRACE - GRATITUDE

STRESS	ENERGY	RECOVERY
On a scale from 1-10 (1= low stress 10 = high stress) Circle One:	On a scale from 1-10 (1= low energy 10 = high energy) Circle One:	In the past 24 Hours
1 2 3	1 2 3	I slept for _____ hours
4 5 6 7	**4 5 6 7**	I napped for _____ min.
8 9 10	**8 9 10**	I practiced mindfulness for _____ min.

HOW DO I FEEL TODAY?

_____

_____

_____

GRATITUDE (I HAVE) — List recent small wins, things your experienced that made you happy, or what you are excited about.

_____

_____

_____

AFFIRMATIONS (I AM) — Give yourself positive self-talk. What actions have supported these affirmations?

_____

_____

_____

INTENTION (I WILL) — What is one area of your performance that you will focus on and/or try to execute?

_____

_____

BE PRESENT • BE AUTHENTIC • GROW DAILY

THOUGHTS	FOCUS	PROCESS
How was my self -talk today? Circle One: POSITIVE **NEUTRAL** NEGATIVE	How was my focus today? Add up to 100% : PAST: ___% **PRESENT: __%** FUTURE: ___%	Did I commit to my plan? **Y/N** Did I seek feedback? **Y/N**

WHAT I DID WELL:

_____

WHAT I LEARNED:

_____

WHAT I WILL WORK ON TO IMPROVE:

_____

OTHER THOUGHTS:

_____

BE WHERE YOUR FEET ARE

STRESS	ENERGY	RECOVERY
On a scale from 1-10 (1= low stress 10 = high stress) Circle One:	On a scale from 1-10 (1= low energy 10 = high energy) Circle One:	In the past 24 Hours
1 2 3 **4 5 6 7** 8 9 10	1 2 3 **4 5 6 7** **8 9 10**	I slept for _____ hours I napped for _____ min. I practiced mindfulness for _____ min.

HOW DO I FEEL TODAY?

_____

_____

_____

GRATITUDE (I HAVE) — List recent small wins, things your experienced that made you happy, or what you are excited about.

_____

_____

_____

AFFIRMATIONS (I AM) — Give yourself positive self-talk. What actions have supported these affirmations?

_____

_____

_____

INTENTION (I WILL) — What is one area of your performance that you will focus on and/or try to execute?

_____

_____

BE PRESENT · BE AUTHENTIC · GROW DAILY

THOUGHTS	FOCUS	PROCESS
How was my self-talk today? Circle One: POSITIVE NEUTRAL NEGATIVE	How was my focus today? Add up to 100% : PAST: __% PRESENT: __% FUTURE: __%	Did I commit to my plan? Y/N Did I seek feedback? Y/N

WHAT I DID WELL:

_____
_____
_____

WHAT I LEARNED:

_____
_____
_____

WHAT I WILL WORK ON TO IMPROVE:

_____
_____
_____

OTHER THOUGHTS:

_____
_____
_____

DO THINGS WITH PURPOSE, ON PURPOSE

STRESS	**ENERGY**	**RECOVERY**
On a scale from 1-10	On a scale from 1-10	In the past 24 Hours
(1= low stress 10 = high stress)	(1= low energy 10 = high energy)	
Circle One:	Circle One:	I slept for _____ hours
1 2 3	1 2 3	I napped for _____ min.
4 5 6 7	**4 5 6 7**	I practiced mindfulness
8 9 10	**8 9 10**	for _____ min.

HOW DO I FEEL TODAY?

_____

_____

_____

GRATITUDE (I HAVE) — List recent small wins, things your experienced that made you happy, or what you are excited about.

_____

_____

_____

AFFIRMATIONS (I AM) — Give yourself positive self-talk. What actions have supported these affirmations?

_____

_____

_____

INTENTION (I WILL) — What is one area of your performance that you will focus on and/or try to execute?

_____

_____

BE PRESENT • BE AUTHENTIC • GROW DAILY

THOUGHTS	FOCUS	PROCESS
How was my self -talk today? Circle One:	How was my focus today? Add up to 100% :	Did I commit to my plan? **Y/N**
POSITIVE **NEUTRAL** NEGATIVE	PAST: ___% **PRESENT: __%** FUTURE: ___%	Did I seek feedback? **Y/N**

WHAT I DID WELL:

_____

_____

_____

WHAT I LEARNED:

_____

_____

_____

WHAT I WILL WORK ON TO IMPROVE:

_____

_____

_____

OTHER THOUGHTS:

_____

_____

_____

W.I.N. STANDS FOR:
WHAT'S IMPORTANT NOW

STRESS	ENERGY	RECOVERY
On a scale from 1-10 (1= low stress 10 = high stress) Circle One:	On a scale from 1-10 (1= low energy 10 = high energy) Circle One:	In the past 24 Hours
1 2 3 **4 5 6 7** 8 9 10	1 2 3 **4 5 6 7** **8 9 10**	I slept for _____ hours I napped for _____ min. I practiced mindfulness for _____ min.

HOW DO I FEEL TODAY?

_____

_____

_____

GRATITUDE (I HAVE) — List recent small wins, things your experienced that made you happy, or what you are excited about.

_____

_____

_____

AFFIRMATIONS (I AM) — Give yourself positive self-talk. What actions have supported these affirmations?

_____

_____

_____

INTENTION (I WILL) — What is one area of your performance that you will focus on and/or try to execute?

_____

_____

BE PRESENT • BE AUTHENTIC • GROW DAILY

THOUGHTS	**FOCUS**	**PROCESS**
How was my self -talk today? Circle One:	How was my focus today? Add up to 100% :	Did I commit to my plan? **Y/N**
POSITIVE **NEUTRAL** **NEGATIVE**	**PAST: ___%** **PRESENT: __%** **FUTURE: __%**	Did I seek feedback? **Y/N**

WHAT I DID WELL:

_____
_____
_____

WHAT I LEARNED:

_____
_____
_____

WHAT I WILL WORK ON TO IMPROVE:

_____
_____
_____

OTHER THOUGHTS:

_____
_____
_____

**DOES THE ROOM LIGHT UP
WHEN YOU ENTER OR WHEN YOU LEAVE?**

STRESS	**ENERGY**	**RECOVERY**
On a scale from 1-10	On a scale from 1-10	In the past 24 Hours
(1= low stress 10 = high stress)	(1= low energy 10 = high energy)	I slept for _____ hours
Circle One:	Circle One:	I napped for _____ min.
1 2 3	1 2 3	I practiced mindfulness
4 5 6 7	**4 5 6 7**	for _____ min.
8 9 10	**8 9 10**	

HOW DO I FEEL TODAY?

_____

_____

_____

GRATITUDE (I HAVE) — List recent small wins, things your experienced that made you happy, or what you are excited about.

_____

_____

_____

AFFIRMATIONS (I AM) — Give yourself positive self-talk. What actions have supported these affirmations?

_____

_____

_____

INTENTION (I WILL) — What is one area of your performance that you will focus on and/or try to execute?

_____

_____

BE PRESENT • BE AUTHENTIC • GROW DAILY

THOUGHTS	FOCUS	PROCESS
How was my self-talk today? Circle One:	How was my focus today? Add up to 100% :	Did I commit to my plan?
POSITIVE	PAST: __%	Y/N
NEUTRAL	PRESENT: __%	Did I seek feedback?
NEGATIVE	FUTURE: __%	Y/N

WHAT I DID WELL:

_____

_____

_____

WHAT I LEARNED:

_____

_____

_____

WHAT I WILL WORK ON TO IMPROVE:

_____

_____

_____

OTHER THOUGHTS:

_____

_____

_____

**THOUGHTS INFLUENCE HOW WE FEEL.
HOW WE FEEL INFLUENCES HOW WE PERFORM.**

STRESS	ENERGY	RECOVERY
On a scale from 1-10	On a scale from 1-10	In the past 24 Hours
(1= low stress 10 = high stress)	(1= low energy 10 = high energy)	I slept for _____ hours
Circle One:	Circle One:	I napped for _____ min.
1 2 3	1 2 3	I practiced mindfulness
4 5 6 7	**4 5 6 7**	for _____ min.
8 9 10	**8 9 10**	

HOW DO I FEEL TODAY?

_____

_____

_____

GRATITUDE (I HAVE) — List recent small wins, things your experienced that made you happy, or what you are excited about.

_____

_____

_____

AFFIRMATIONS (I AM) — Give yourself positive self-talk. What actions have supported these affirmations?

_____

_____

_____

INTENTION (I WILL) — What is one area of your performance that you will focus on and/or try to execute?

_____

_____

BE PRESENT · BE AUTHENTIC · GROW DAILY

THOUGHTS	FOCUS	PROCESS
How was my self -talk today? Circle One:	How was my focus today? Add up to 100% :	Did I commit to my plan? **Y/N**
POSITIVE **NEUTRAL** NEGATIVE	PAST: ___% **PRESENT: __%** FUTURE: ___%	Did I seek feedback? **Y/N**

WHAT I DID WELL:

_____

_____

_____

WHAT I LEARNED:

_____

_____

_____

WHAT I WILL WORK ON TO IMPROVE:

_____

_____

_____

OTHER THOUGHTS:

_____

_____

_____

COURAGE COMES BEFORE CONFIDENCE

STRESS	ENERGY	RECOVERY
On a scale from 1-10	On a scale from 1-10	In the past 24 Hours
(1= low stress 10 = high stress)	(1= low energy 10 = high energy)	I slept for _____ hours
Circle One:	Circle One:	I napped for _____ min.
1 2 3	1 2 3	I practiced mindfulness
4 5 6 7	**4 5 6 7**	for _____ min.
8 9 10	**8 9 10**	

HOW DO I FEEL TODAY?

_____

_____

_____

GRATITUDE (I HAVE) — List recent small wins, things your experienced that made you happy, or what you are excited about.

_____

_____

_____

AFFIRMATIONS (I AM) — Give yourself positive self-talk. What actions have supported these affirmations?

_____

_____

_____

INTENTION (I WILL) — What is one area of your performance that you will focus on and/or try to execute?

_____

_____

BE PRESENT • BE AUTHENTIC • GROW DAILY

THOUGHTS	FOCUS	PROCESS
How was my self -talk today? Circle One:	How was my focus today? Add up to 100% :	Did I commit to my plan?
POSITIVE		**Y / N**
NEUTRAL	PAST: ___%	Did I seek feedback?
NEGATIVE	**PRESENT: ___%**	**Y / N**
	FUTURE: ___%	

WHAT I DID WELL:

_____

_____

_____

WHAT I LEARNED:

_____

_____

_____

WHAT I WILL WORK ON TO IMPROVE:

_____

_____

_____

OTHER THOUGHTS:

_____

_____

_____

THERE ARE TWO PAINS IN LIFE: THE PAIN OF REGRET AND THE PAIN OF HARD WORK.

STRESS	**ENERGY**	**RECOVERY**
On a scale from 1-10	On a scale from 1-10	In the past 24 Hours
(1= low stress 10 = high stress)	(1= low energy 10 = high energy)	
Circle One:	Circle One:	I slept for _____ hours
1 2 3	1 2 3	I napped for _____ min.
4 5 6 7	**4 5 6 7**	I practiced mindfulness
8 9 10	**8 9 10**	for _____ min.

HOW DO I FEEL TODAY?

_____

_____

_____

GRATITUDE (I HAVE) — List recent small wins, things your experienced that made you happy, or what you are excited about.

_____

_____

_____

AFFIRMATIONS (I AM) — Give yourself positive self-talk. What actions have supported these affirmations?

_____

_____

_____

INTENTION (I WILL) — What is one area of your performance that you will focus on and/or try to execute?

_____

_____

BE PRESENT • BE AUTHENTIC • GROW DAILY

THOUGHTS	FOCUS	PROCESS
How was my self-talk today? Circle One:	How was my focus today? Add up to 100% :	Did I commit to my plan?
POSITIVE		Y/N
NEUTRAL	PAST: ___%	Did I seek feedback?
NEGATIVE	PRESENT: __%	Y/N
	FUTURE: ___%	

WHAT I DID WELL:

_____

_____

_____

WHAT I LEARNED:

_____

_____

_____

WHAT I WILL WORK ON TO IMPROVE:

_____

_____

_____

OTHER THOUGHTS:

_____

_____

_____

FOCUS ON THE PROCESS NOT THE PRIZE

STRESS	**ENERGY**	**RECOVERY**
On a scale from 1-10	On a scale from 1-10	In the past 24 Hours
(1= low stress 10 = high stress)	(1= low energy 10 = high energy)	I slept for _____ hours
Circle One:	Circle One:	I napped for _____ min.
1 2 3	1 2 3	I practiced mindfulness
4 5 6 7	**4 5 6 7**	for _____ min.
8 9 10	**8 9 10**	

HOW DO I FEEL TODAY?

_____

_____

_____

GRATITUDE (I HAVE) — List recent small wins, things your experienced that made you happy, or what you are excited about.

_____

_____

_____

AFFIRMATIONS (I AM) — Give yourself positive self-talk. What actions have supported these affirmations?

_____

_____

_____

INTENTION (I WILL) — What is one area of your performance that you will focus on and/or try to execute?

_____

_____

BE PRESENT · BE AUTHENTIC · GROW DAILY

THOUGHTS	**FOCUS**	**PROCESS**
How was my self-talk today? Circle One:	How was my focus today? Add up to 100% :	Did I commit to my plan?
POSITIVE	PAST: __%	**Y/N**
NEUTRAL	**PRESENT: __%**	Did I seek feedback?
NEGATIVE	FUTURE: __%	**Y/N**

WHAT I DID WELL:

_____
_____
_____

WHAT I LEARNED:

_____
_____
_____

WHAT I WILL WORK ON TO IMPROVE:

_____
_____
_____

OTHER THOUGHTS:

_____
_____
_____

WORRYING IS BETTING AGAINST YOURSELF

STRESS	**ENERGY**	**RECOVERY**
On a scale from 1-10	On a scale from 1-10	In the past 24 Hours
(1= low stress 10 = high stress)	(1= low energy 10 = high energy)	
Circle One:	Circle One:	I slept for _____ hours
1 2 3	1 2 3	I napped for _____ min.
4 5 6 7	**4 5 6 7**	I practiced mindfulness
8 9 10	**8 9 10**	for _____ min.

HOW DO I FEEL TODAY?

_____

_____

_____

GRATITUDE (I HAVE) — List recent small wins, things your experienced that made you happy, or what you are excited about.

_____

_____

_____

AFFIRMATIONS (I AM) — Give yourself positive self-talk. What actions have supported these affirmations?

_____

_____

_____

INTENTION (I WILL) — What is one area of your performance that you will focus on and/or try to execute?

_____

_____

BE PRESENT • BE AUTHENTIC • GROW DAILY

THOUGHTS	FOCUS	PROCESS
How was my self-talk today? Circle One:	How was my focus today? Add up to 100% :	Did I commit to my plan? **Y / N**
POSITIVE **NEUTRAL** **NEGATIVE**	**PAST: __%** **PRESENT: __%** **FUTURE: __%**	Did I seek feedback? **Y / N**

WHAT I DID WELL:

_____
_____
_____

WHAT I LEARNED:

_____
_____
_____

WHAT I WILL WORK ON TO IMPROVE:

_____
_____
_____

OTHER THOUGHTS:

_____
_____
_____

WE RISE BY HELPING OTHERS

STRESS	**ENERGY**	**RECOVERY**
On a scale from 1-10	On a scale from 1-10	In the past 24 Hours
(1= low stress 10 = high stress)	(1= low energy 10 = high energy)	I slept for _____ hours
Circle One:	Circle One:	I napped for _____ min.
1 2 3	1 2 3	I practiced mindfulness
4 5 6 7	**4 5 6 7**	for _____ min.
8 9 10	**8 9 10**	

HOW DO I FEEL TODAY?

_____

_____

_____

GRATITUDE (I HAVE) — List recent small wins, things your experienced that made you happy, or what you are excited about.

_____

_____

_____

AFFIRMATIONS (I AM) — Give yourself positive self-talk. What actions have supported these affirmations?

_____

_____

_____

INTENTION (I WILL) — What is one area of your performance that you will focus on and/or try to execute?

_____

_____

BE PRESENT · BE AUTHENTIC · GROW DAILY

THOUGHTS	FOCUS	PROCESS
How was my self-talk today? Circle One:	How was my focus today? Add up to 100% :	Did I commit to my plan?
POSITIVE	PAST: __%	**Y/N**
NEUTRAL	**PRESENT: __%**	Did I seek feedback?
NEGATIVE	FUTURE: __%	**Y/N**

WHAT I DID WELL:

_____

_____

_____

WHAT I LEARNED:

_____

_____

_____

WHAT I WILL WORK ON TO IMPROVE:

_____

_____

_____

OTHER THOUGHTS:

_____

_____

_____

YOU WERE DESIGNED FOR A REASON

PRE-FLOW   DATE:

STRESS	ENERGY	RECOVERY
On a scale from 1-10 (1= low stress 10 = high stress) Circle One:	On a scale from 1-10 (1= low energy 10 = high energy) Circle One:	In the past 24 Hours
1 2 3	1 2 3	I slept for _____ hours
4 5 6 7	**4 5 6 7**	I napped for _____ min.
8 9 10	**8 9 10**	I practiced mindfulness for _____ min.

HOW DO I FEEL TODAY?

_____

_____

_____

GRATITUDE (I HAVE) — List recent small wins, things your experienced that made you happy, or what you are excited about.

_____

_____

_____

AFFIRMATIONS (I AM) — Give yourself positive self-talk. What actions have supported these affirmations?

_____

_____

_____

INTENTION (I WILL) — What is one area of your performance that you will focus on and/or try to execute?

_____

_____

BE PRESENT · BE AUTHENTIC · GROW DAILY

| **THOUGHTS**
How was my
self -talk today?
Circle One:

POSITIVE
NEUTRAL
NEGATIVE | **FOCUS**
How was my focus today?
Add up to 100% :

PAST: __%
PRESENT: __%
FUTURE: __% | **PROCESS**
Did I commit to my plan?
Y/N

Did I seek feedback?
Y/N |

WHAT I DID WELL:

_____
_____
_____

WHAT I LEARNED:

_____
_____
_____

WHAT I WILL WORK ON TO IMPROVE:

_____
_____
_____

OTHER THOUGHTS:

_____
_____
_____

**CLUTCH MEANS DOING WHAT YOU NORMALLY
CAN DO WHEN IT MATTERS MOST**

STRESS	ENERGY	RECOVERY
On a scale from 1-10	On a scale from 1-10	In the past 24 Hours
(1= low stress 10 = high stress)	(1= low energy 10 = high energy)	
Circle One:	Circle One:	I slept for _____ hours
1 2 3	1 2 3	I napped for _____ min.
4 5 6 7	**4 5 6 7**	I practiced mindfulness
8 9 10	**8 9 10**	for _____ min.

HOW DO I FEEL TODAY?

_____

_____

_____

GRATITUDE (I HAVE) — List recent small wins, things your experienced that made you happy, or what you are excited about.

_____

_____

_____

AFFIRMATIONS (I AM) — Give yourself positive self-talk. What actions have supported these affirmations?

_____

_____

_____

INTENTION (I WILL) — What is one area of your performance that you will focus on and/or try to execute?

_____

_____

BE PRESENT • BE AUTHENTIC • GROW DAILY

THOUGHTS	**FOCUS**	**PROCESS**
How was my self -talk today? Circle One:	How was my focus today? Add up to 100% :	Did I commit to my plan?
POSITIVE	PAST: __%	**Y / N**
NEUTRAL	**PRESENT: __%**	Did I seek feedback?
NEGATIVE	FUTURE: __%	**Y / N**

WHAT I DID WELL:

_____

_____

_____

WHAT I LEARNED:

_____

_____

_____

WHAT I WILL WORK ON TO IMPROVE:

_____

_____

_____

OTHER THOUGHTS:

_____

_____

_____

WE DON'T RISE TO THE OCCASION - WE RISE TO OUR TRAINING

STRESS	ENERGY	RECOVERY
On a scale from 1-10	On a scale from 1-10	In the past 24 Hours
(1= low stress 10 = high stress)	(1= low energy 10 = high energy)	
Circle One:	Circle One:	I slept for _____ hours
1 2 3	1 2 3	I napped for _____ min.
4 5 6 7	**4 5 6 7**	I practiced mindfulness
8 9 10	**8 9 10**	for _____ min.

HOW DO I FEEL TODAY?

_____

_____

_____

GRATITUDE (I HAVE) — List recent small wins, things your experienced that made you happy, or what you are excited about.

_____

_____

_____

AFFIRMATIONS (I AM) — Give yourself positive self-talk. What actions have supported these affirmations?

_____

_____

_____

INTENTION (I WILL) — What is one area of your performance that you will focus on and/or try to execute?

_____

_____

BE PRESENT • BE AUTHENTIC • GROW DAILY

THOUGHTS	FOCUS	PROCESS
How was my self-talk today? Circle One:	How was my focus today? Add up to 100% :	Did I commit to my plan? **Y/N**
POSITIVE **NEUTRAL** NEGATIVE	PAST: __% **PRESENT: __%** FUTURE: __%	Did I seek feedback? **Y/N**

WHAT I DID WELL:

_____
_____
_____

WHAT I LEARNED:

_____
_____
_____

WHAT I WILL WORK ON TO IMPROVE:

_____
_____
_____

OTHER THOUGHTS:

_____
_____
_____

WHATEVER THE BRAIN CAN CONCEIVE AND BELIEVE, IT CAN ACHIEVE

STRESS	ENERGY	RECOVERY
On a scale from 1-10	On a scale from 1-10	In the past 24 Hours
(1= low stress 10 = high stress)	(1= low energy 10 = high energy)	I slept for _____ hours
Circle One:	Circle One:	I napped for _____ min.
1 2 3	1 2 3	I practiced mindfulness
4 5 6 7	**4 5 6 7**	for _____ min.
8 9 10	**8 9 10**	

HOW DO I FEEL TODAY?

_____

_____

_____

GRATITUDE (I HAVE) — List recent small wins, things your experienced that made you happy, or what you are excited about.

_____

_____

_____

AFFIRMATIONS (I AM) — Give yourself positive self-talk. What actions have supported these affirmations?

_____

_____

_____

INTENTION (I WILL) — What is one area of your performance that you will focus on and/or try to execute?

_____

_____

BE PRESENT · BE AUTHENTIC · GROW DAILY

THOUGHTS	**FOCUS**	**PROCESS**
How was my self-talk today? Circle One:	How was my focus today? Add up to 100% :	Did I commit to my plan?
POSITIVE	PAST: __%	**Y/N**
NEUTRAL	**PRESENT: __%**	Did I seek feedback?
NEGATIVE	FUTURE: __%	**Y/N**

WHAT I DID WELL:

_____

_____

_____

WHAT I LEARNED:

_____

_____

_____

WHAT I WILL WORK ON TO IMPROVE:

_____

_____

_____

OTHER THOUGHTS:

_____

_____

_____

NO ONE SHOULD WIN OR WORRY ALONE

STRESS	**ENERGY**	**RECOVERY**
On a scale from 1-10	On a scale from 1-10	In the past 24 Hours
(1= low stress 10 = high stress)	(1= low energy 10 = high energy)	
Circle One:	Circle One:	I slept for _____ hours
1 2 3	1 2 3	I napped for _____ min.
4 5 6 7	**4 5 6 7**	I practiced mindfulness
8 9 10	**8 9 10**	for _____ min.

HOW DO I FEEL TODAY?

_____

_____

_____

GRATITUDE (I HAVE) — List recent small wins, things your experienced that made you happy, or what you are excited about.

_____

_____

_____

AFFIRMATIONS (I AM) — Give yourself positive self-talk. What actions have supported these affirmations?

_____

_____

_____

INTENTION (I WILL) — What is one area of your performance that you will focus on and/or try to execute?

_____

_____

BE PRESENT • BE AUTHENTIC • GROW DAILY

THOUGHTS

How was my
self -talk today?
Circle One:

POSITIVE
NEUTRAL
NEGATIVE

FOCUS

How was my focus today?
Add up to 100% :

PAST: __%
PRESENT: __%
FUTURE: __%

PROCESS

Did I commit to my plan?

Y/N

Did I seek feedback?

Y/N

WHAT I DID WELL:

_____
_____
_____

WHAT I LEARNED:

_____
_____
_____

WHAT I WILL WORK ON TO IMPROVE:

_____
_____
_____

OTHER THOUGHTS:

_____
_____
_____

GO THE EXTRA MILE - IT'S NEVER CROWDED

STRESS	**ENERGY**	**RECOVERY**
On a scale from 1-10	On a scale from 1-10	In the past 24 Hours
(1= low stress 10 = high stress)	(1= low energy 10 = high energy)	
Circle One:	Circle One:	I slept for _____ hours
1 2 3	1 2 3	I napped for _____ min.
4 5 6 7	**4 5 6 7**	I practiced mindfulness
8 9 10	**8 9 10**	for _____ min.

HOW DO I FEEL TODAY?

_____

_____

_____

GRATITUDE (I HAVE) — List recent small wins, things your experienced that made you happy, or what you are excited about.

_____

_____

_____

AFFIRMATIONS (I AM) — Give yourself positive self-talk. What actions have supported these affirmations?

_____

_____

_____

INTENTION (I WILL) — What is one area of your performance that you will focus on and/or try to execute?

_____

_____

BE PRESENT • BE AUTHENTIC • GROW DAILY

THOUGHTS	FOCUS	PROCESS
How was my self -talk today? Circle One:	How was my focus today? Add up to 100% :	Did I commit to my plan?
POSITIVE		**Y/N**
NEUTRAL	**PAST: __%**	Did I seek feedback?
NEGATIVE	**PRESENT: __%**	**Y/N**
	FUTURE: __%	

WHAT I DID WELL:

_____

_____

_____

WHAT I LEARNED:

_____

_____

_____

WHAT I WILL WORK ON TO IMPROVE:

_____

_____

_____

OTHER THOUGHTS:

_____

_____

_____

ENERGY FLOWS WHERE FOCUS GOES

STRESS	**ENERGY**	**RECOVERY**
On a scale from 1-10	On a scale from 1-10	In the past 24 Hours
(1= low stress 10 = high stress)	(1= low energy 10 = high energy)	
Circle One:	Circle One:	I slept for _____ hours
1 2 3	1 2 3	I napped for _____ min.
4 5 6 7	**4 5 6 7**	I practiced mindfulness
8 9 10	**8 9 10**	for _____ min.

HOW DO I FEEL TODAY?

_____

_____

_____

GRATITUDE (I HAVE) — List recent small wins, things your experienced that made you happy, or what you are excited about.

_____

_____

_____

AFFIRMATIONS (I AM) — Give yourself positive self-talk. What actions have supported these affirmations?

_____

_____

_____

INTENTION (I WILL) — What is one area of your performance that you will focus on and/or try to execute?

_____

_____

BE PRESENT · BE AUTHENTIC · GROW DAILY

THOUGHTS	**FOCUS**	**PROCESS**
How was my self-talk today? Circle One:	How was my focus today? Add up to 100% :	Did I commit to my plan? **Y/N**
POSITIVE **NEUTRAL** NEGATIVE	PAST: __% **PRESENT: __%** FUTURE: __%	Did I seek feedback? **Y/N**

WHAT I DID WELL:

_____

_____

_____

WHAT I LEARNED:

_____

_____

_____

WHAT I WILL WORK ON TO IMPROVE:

_____

_____

_____

OTHER THOUGHTS:

_____

_____

_____

HOW CAN YOU BECOME WHAT YOU DON'T BELIEVE?

STRESS	ENERGY	RECOVERY
On a scale from 1-10	On a scale from 1-10	In the past 24 Hours
(1= low stress 10 = high stress)	(1= low energy 10 = high energy)	
Circle One:	Circle One:	I slept for _____ hours
1 2 3	1 2 3	I napped for _____ min.
4 5 6 7	**4 5 6 7**	I practiced mindfulness
8 9 10	**8 9 10**	for _____ min.

HOW DO I FEEL TODAY?

_____

_____

_____

GRATITUDE (I HAVE) — List recent small wins, things your experienced that made you happy, or what you are excited about.

_____

_____

_____

AFFIRMATIONS (I AM) — Give yourself positive self-talk. What actions have supported these affirmations?

_____

_____

_____

INTENTION (I WILL) — What is one area of your performance that you will focus on and/or try to execute?

_____

_____

BE PRESENT · BE AUTHENTIC · GROW DAILY

THOUGHTS	FOCUS	PROCESS
How was my self-talk today? Circle One: POSITIVE NEUTRAL NEGATIVE	How was my focus today? Add up to 100%: PAST: __% PRESENT: __% FUTURE: __%	Did I commit to my plan? Y/N Did I seek feedback? Y/N

WHAT I DID WELL:

_____

_____

_____

WHAT I LEARNED:

_____

_____

_____

WHAT I WILL WORK ON TO IMPROVE:

_____

_____

_____

OTHER THOUGHTS:

_____

_____

_____

QUALITY THOUGHT = QUALITY MOVEMENT

STRESS	ENERGY	RECOVERY
On a scale from 1-10	On a scale from 1-10	In the past 24 Hours
(1= low stress 10 = high stress)	(1= low energy 10 = high energy)	
Circle One:	Circle One:	I slept for _____ hours
1 2 3	1 2 3	I napped for _____ min.
4 5 6 7	**4 5 6 7**	I practiced mindfulness
8 9 10	**8 9 10**	for _____ min.

HOW DO I FEEL TODAY?

_____

_____

_____

GRATITUDE (I HAVE) — List recent small wins, things your experienced that made you happy, or what you are excited about.

_____

_____

_____

AFFIRMATIONS (I AM) — Give yourself positive self-talk. What actions have supported these affirmations?

_____

_____

_____

INTENTION (I WILL) — What is one area of your performance that you will focus on and/or try to execute?

_____

_____

BE PRESENT · BE AUTHENTIC · GROW DAILY

THOUGHTS	FOCUS	PROCESS
How was my self-talk today? Circle One: **POSITIVE NEUTRAL NEGATIVE**	How was my focus today? Add up to 100% : **PAST: __% PRESENT: __% FUTURE: __%**	Did I commit to my plan? **Y/N** Did I seek feedback? **Y/N**

WHAT I DID WELL:

_____
_____
_____

WHAT I LEARNED:

_____
_____
_____

WHAT I WILL WORK ON TO IMPROVE:

_____
_____
_____

OTHER THOUGHTS:

_____
_____
_____

JUST BE YOU

STRESS	ENERGY	RECOVERY
On a scale from 1-10 (1= low stress 10 = high stress) Circle One:	On a scale from 1-10 (1= low energy 10 = high energy) Circle One:	In the past 24 Hours
1 2 3 **4 5 6 7** 8 9 10	1 2 3 **4 5 6 7** **8 9 10**	I slept for _____ hours I napped for _____ min. I practiced mindfulness for _____ min.

HOW DO I FEEL TODAY?

_____

_____

_____

GRATITUDE (I HAVE) — List recent small wins, things your experienced that made you happy, or what you are excited about.

_____

_____

_____

AFFIRMATIONS (I AM) — Give yourself positive self-talk. What actions have supported these affirmations?

_____

_____

_____

INTENTION (I WILL) — What is one area of your performance that you will focus on and/or try to execute?

_____

_____

BE PRESENT • BE AUTHENTIC • GROW DAILY

THOUGHTS
How was my
self -talk today?
Circle One:

POSITIVE
NEUTRAL
NEGATIVE

FOCUS
How was my focus today?
Add up to 100% :

PAST: __%
PRESENT: __%
FUTURE: __%

PROCESS
Did I commit to my plan?

Y/N

Did I seek feedback?

Y/N

WHAT I DID WELL:

_____
_____
_____

WHAT I LEARNED:

_____
_____
_____

WHAT I WILL WORK ON TO IMPROVE:

_____
_____
_____

OTHER THOUGHTS:

_____
_____
_____

MORE ISN'T BETTER - BETTER IS BETTER

STRESS	**ENERGY**	**RECOVERY**
On a scale from 1-10	On a scale from 1-10	In the past 24 Hours
(1= low stress 10 = high stress)	(1= low energy 10 = high energy)	
Circle One:	Circle One:	I slept for _____ hours
1 2 3	1 2 3	I napped for _____ min.
4 5 6 7	**4 5 6 7**	I practiced mindfulness
8 9 10	**8 9 10**	for _____ min.

HOW DO I FEEL TODAY?

_____

_____

_____

GRATITUDE (I HAVE) — List recent small wins, things your experienced that made you happy, or what you are excited about.

_____

_____

_____

AFFIRMATIONS (I AM) — Give yourself positive self-talk. What actions have supported these affirmations?

_____

_____

_____

INTENTION (I WILL) — What is one area of your performance that you will focus on and/or try to execute?

_____

_____

BE PRESENT · BE AUTHENTIC · GROW DAILY

THOUGHTS	**FOCUS**	**PROCESS**
How was my self -talk today? Circle One:	How was my focus today? Add up to 100% :	Did I commit to my plan?
POSITIVE	PAST: __%	**Y/N**
NEUTRAL	**PRESENT: __%**	Did I seek feedback?
NEGATIVE	FUTURE: __%	**Y/N**

WHAT I DID WELL:

_____

_____

_____

WHAT I LEARNED:

_____

_____

_____

WHAT I WILL WORK ON TO IMPROVE:

_____

_____

_____

OTHER THOUGHTS:

_____

_____

_____

WHAT YOU DO IN THE DARK
SHINES BRIGHT IN THE LIGHT

STRESS	**ENERGY**	**RECOVERY**
On a scale from 1-10	On a scale from 1-10	In the past 24 Hours
(1= low stress 10 = high stress)	(1= low energy 10 = high energy)	
Circle One:	Circle One:	I slept for _____ hours
1 2 3	1 2 3	I napped for _____ min.
4 5 6 7	**4 5 6 7**	I practiced mindfulness
8 9 10	**8 9 10**	for _____ min.

HOW DO I FEEL TODAY?

_____

_____

_____

GRATITUDE (I HAVE) — List recent small wins, things your experienced that made you happy, or what you are excited about.

_____

_____

_____

AFFIRMATIONS (I AM) — Give yourself positive self-talk. What actions have supported these affirmations?

_____

_____

_____

INTENTION (I WILL) — What is one area of your performance that you will focus on and/or try to execute?

_____

_____

BE PRESENT • BE AUTHENTIC • GROW DAILY

THOUGHTS	FOCUS	PROCESS
How was my self -talk today? Circle One:	How was my focus today? Add up to 100% :	Did I commit to my plan?
POSITIVE	PAST: __%	Y/N
NEUTRAL	**PRESENT: __%**	Did I seek feedback?
NEGATIVE	FUTURE: __%	Y/N

WHAT I DID WELL:

_____

_____

_____

WHAT I LEARNED:

_____

_____

_____

WHAT I WILL WORK ON TO IMPROVE:

_____

_____

_____

OTHER THOUGHTS:

_____

_____

_____

TRUST YOUR TRAINING

PRE-FLOW   DATE:

STRESS	**ENERGY**	**RECOVERY**
On a scale from 1-10	On a scale from 1-10	In the past 24 Hours
(1= low stress 10 = high stress)	(1= low energy 10 = high energy)	
Circle One:	Circle One:	I slept for _____ hours
1 2 3	1 2 3	I napped for _____ min.
4 5 6 7	**4 5 6 7**	I practiced mindfulness
8 9 10	**8 9 10**	for _____ min.

HOW DO I FEEL TODAY?

_____

_____

_____

GRATITUDE (I HAVE) — List recent small wins, things your experienced that made you happy, or what you are excited about.

_____

_____

_____

AFFIRMATIONS (I AM) — Give yourself positive self-talk. What actions have supported these affirmations?

_____

_____

_____

INTENTION (I WILL) — What is one area of your performance that you will focus on and/or try to execute?

_____

_____

BE PRESENT · BE AUTHENTIC · GROW DAILY

THOUGHTS	FOCUS	PROCESS
How was my self-talk today? Circle One:	How was my focus today? Add up to 100% :	Did I commit to my plan?
POSITIVE		**Y/N**
NEUTRAL	**PAST:** ___%	Did I seek feedback?
NEGATIVE	**PRESENT:** __%	**Y/N**
	FUTURE: ___%	

WHAT I DID WELL:

_____

_____

_____

WHAT I LEARNED:

_____

_____

_____

WHAT I WILL WORK ON TO IMPROVE:

_____

_____

_____

OTHER THOUGHTS:

_____

_____

_____

THE MOST IMPORTANT MOMENT IS ALWAYS NOW

STRESS	**ENERGY**	**RECOVERY**
On a scale from 1-10	On a scale from 1-10	In the past 24 Hours
(1= low stress 10 = high stress)	(1= low energy 10 = high energy)	
Circle One:	Circle One:	I slept for _____ hours
1 2 3	1 2 3	I napped for _____ min.
4 5 6 7	**4 5 6 7**	I practiced mindfulness
8 9 10	**8 9 10**	for _____ min.

HOW DO I FEEL TODAY?

_____

_____

_____

GRATITUDE (I HAVE) — List recent small wins, things your experienced that made you happy, or what you are excited about.

_____

_____

_____

AFFIRMATIONS (I AM) — Give yourself positive self-talk. What actions have supported these affirmations?

_____

_____

_____

INTENTION (I WILL) — What is one area of your performance that you will focus on and/or try to execute?

_____

_____

BE PRESENT · BE AUTHENTIC · GROW DAILY

THOUGHTS
How was my self-talk today?
Circle One:

POSITIVE
NEUTRAL
NEGATIVE

FOCUS
How was my focus today?
Add up to 100%:

PAST: __%
PRESENT: __%
FUTURE: __%

PROCESS
Did I commit to my plan?

Y/N

Did I seek feedback?

Y/N

WHAT I DID WELL:

_____
_____
_____

WHAT I LEARNED:

_____
_____
_____

WHAT I WILL WORK ON TO IMPROVE:

_____
_____
_____

OTHER THOUGHTS:

_____
_____
_____

FOCUS ON THE PROCESS NOT THE PRESSURE

STRESS	ENERGY	RECOVERY
On a scale from 1-10	On a scale from 1-10	In the past 24 Hours
(1= low stress 10 = high stress)	(1= low energy 10 = high energy)	
Circle One:	Circle One:	I slept for _____ hours
1 2 3	1 2 3	I napped for _____ min.
4 5 6 7	**4 5 6 7**	I practiced mindfulness
8 9 10	**8 9 10**	for _____ min.

HOW DO I FEEL TODAY?

_____

_____

_____

GRATITUDE (I HAVE) — List recent small wins, things your experienced that made you happy, or what you are excited about.

_____

_____

_____

AFFIRMATIONS (I AM) — Give yourself positive self-talk. What actions have supported these affirmations?

_____

_____

_____

INTENTION (I WILL) — What is one area of your performance that you will focus on and/or try to execute?

_____

_____

BE PRESENT • BE AUTHENTIC • GROW DAILY

THOUGHTS	FOCUS	PROCESS
How was my self-talk today? Circle One: **POSITIVE NEUTRAL NEGATIVE**	How was my focus today? Add up to 100%: **PAST: __% PRESENT: __% FUTURE: __%**	Did I commit to my plan? **Y/N** Did I seek feedback? **Y/N**

WHAT I DID WELL:

_____

_____

_____

WHAT I LEARNED:

_____

_____

_____

WHAT I WILL WORK ON TO IMPROVE:

_____

_____

_____

OTHER THOUGHTS:

_____

_____

_____

YOU ARE A BY-PRODUCT OF THE PEOPLE YOU HANG OUT WITH THE MOST...CHOOSE WISELY

STRESS	ENERGY	RECOVERY
On a scale from 1-10	On a scale from 1-10	In the past 24 Hours
(1= low stress 10 = high stress)	(1= low energy 10 = high energy)	
Circle One:	Circle One:	I slept for _____ hours
1 2 3	1 2 3	I napped for _____ min.
4 5 6 7	**4 5 6 7**	I practiced mindfulness
8 9 10	**8 9 10**	for _____ min.

HOW DO I FEEL TODAY?

_____

_____

_____

GRATITUDE (I HAVE) — List recent small wins, things your experienced that made you happy, or what you are excited about.

_____

_____

_____

AFFIRMATIONS (I AM) — Give yourself positive self-talk. What actions have supported these affirmations?

_____

_____

_____

INTENTION (I WILL) — What is one area of your performance that you will focus on and/or try to execute?

_____

_____

BE PRESENT · BE AUTHENTIC · GROW DAILY

THOUGHTS	FOCUS	PROCESS
How was my self -talk today? Circle One: POSITIVE NEUTRAL NEGATIVE	How was my focus today? Add up to 100% : PAST: __% PRESENT: __% FUTURE: __%	Did I commit to my plan? Y/N Did I seek feedback? Y/N

WHAT I DID WELL:

_____

_____

_____

WHAT I LEARNED:

_____

_____

_____

WHAT I WILL WORK ON TO IMPROVE:

_____

_____

_____

OTHER THOUGHTS:

_____

_____

_____

RECOVERY IS JUST AS IMPORTANT AS GRINDING

STRESS	**ENERGY**	**RECOVERY**
On a scale from 1-10	On a scale from 1-10	In the past 24 Hours
(1 = low stress 10 = high stress)	(1 = low energy 10 = high energy)	
Circle One:	Circle One:	I slept for _____ hours
1 2 3	1 2 3	I napped for _____ min.
4 5 6 7	**4 5 6 7**	I practiced mindfulness
8 9 10	**8 9 10**	for _____ min.

HOW DO I FEEL TODAY?

_____

_____

_____

GRATITUDE (I HAVE) — List recent small wins, things your experienced that made you happy, or what you are excited about.

_____

_____

_____

AFFIRMATIONS (I AM) — Give yourself positive self-talk. What actions have supported these affirmations?

_____

_____

_____

INTENTION (I WILL) — What is one area of your performance that you will focus on and/or try to execute?

_____

_____

BE PRESENT • BE AUTHENTIC • GROW DAILY

THOUGHTS	FOCUS	PROCESS
How was my self -talk today? Circle One:	How was my focus today? Add up to 100% :	Did I commit to my plan?
POSITIVE	**PAST: __%**	**Y/N**
NEUTRAL	**PRESENT: __%**	Did I seek feedback?
NEGATIVE	**FUTURE: __%**	**Y/N**

WHAT I DID WELL:

_____

_____

_____

WHAT I LEARNED:

_____

_____

_____

WHAT I WILL WORK ON TO IMPROVE:

_____

_____

_____

OTHER THOUGHTS:

_____

_____

_____

IF YOU DO WHAT YOU FEAR THE MOST, THERE'S NOTHING YOU CANNOT DO

STRESS	**ENERGY**	**RECOVERY**
On a scale from 1-10	On a scale from 1-10	In the past 24 Hours
(1= low stress 10 = high stress)	(1= low energy 10 = high energy)	
Circle One:	Circle One:	I slept for _____ hours
1 2 3	1 2 3	I napped for _____ min.
4 5 6 7	**4 5 6 7**	I practiced mindfulness
8 9 10	**8 9 10**	for _____ min.

HOW DO I FEEL TODAY?

_____

_____

_____

GRATITUDE (I HAVE) — List recent small wins, things your experienced that made you happy, or what you are excited about.

_____

_____

_____

AFFIRMATIONS (I AM) — Give yourself positive self-talk. What actions have supported these affirmations?

_____

_____

_____

INTENTION (I WILL) — What is one area of your performance that you will focus on and/or try to execute?

_____

_____

BE PRESENT • BE AUTHENTIC • GROW DAILY

THOUGHTS

How was my
self -talk today?
Circle One:

POSITIVE
NEUTRAL
NEGATIVE

FOCUS

How was my focus today?
Add up to 100% :

PAST: __%
PRESENT: __%
FUTURE: __%

PROCESS

Did I commit to my plan?

Y/N

Did I seek feedback?

Y/N

WHAT I DID WELL:

_____

_____

_____

WHAT I LEARNED:

_____

_____

_____

WHAT I WILL WORK ON TO IMPROVE:

_____

_____

_____

OTHER THOUGHTS:

_____

_____

_____

TRUE COURAGE IS BEING VULNERABLE

STRESS	**ENERGY**	**RECOVERY**
On a scale from 1-10 (1= low stress 10 = high stress) Circle One:	On a scale from 1-10 (1= low energy 10 = high energy) Circle One:	In the past 24 Hours
1 2 3	1 2 3	I slept for _____ hours
4 5 6 7	**4 5 6 7**	I napped for _____ min.
8 9 10	**8 9 10**	I practiced mindfulness for _____ min.

HOW DO I FEEL TODAY?

_____

_____

_____

GRATITUDE (I HAVE) — List recent small wins, things your experienced that made you happy, or what you are excited about.

_____

_____

_____

AFFIRMATIONS (I AM) — Give yourself positive self-talk. What actions have supported these affirmations?

_____

_____

_____

INTENTION (I WILL) — What is one area of your performance that you will focus on and/or try to execute?

_____

_____

BE PRESENT • BE AUTHENTIC • GROW DAILY

THOUGHTS	FOCUS	PROCESS
How was my self-talk today? Circle One: POSITIVE **NEUTRAL** NEGATIVE	How was my focus today? Add up to 100% : PAST: __% PRESENT: __% FUTURE: __%	Did I commit to my plan? **Y/N** Did I seek feedback? **Y/N**

WHAT I DID WELL:

WHAT I LEARNED:

WHAT I WILL WORK ON TO IMPROVE:

OTHER THOUGHTS:

F.A.I.L. = FIRST ATTEMPT IN LEARNING

STRESS	**ENERGY**	**RECOVERY**
On a scale from 1-10	On a scale from 1-10	In the past 24 Hours
(1= low stress 10 = high stress)	(1= low energy 10 = high energy)	
Circle One:	Circle One:	I slept for _____ hours
1 2 3	1 2 3	I napped for _____ min.
4 5 6 7	**4 5 6 7**	I practiced mindfulness
8 9 10	**8 9 10**	for _____ min.

HOW DO I FEEL TODAY?

_____

_____

_____

GRATITUDE (I HAVE) — List recent small wins, things your experienced that made you happy, or what you are excited about.

_____

_____

_____

AFFIRMATIONS (I AM) — Give yourself positive self-talk. What actions have supported these affirmations?

_____

_____

_____

INTENTION (I WILL) — What is one area of your performance that you will focus on and/or try to execute?

_____

_____

BE PRESENT · BE AUTHENTIC · GROW DAILY

THOUGHTS	**FOCUS**	**PROCESS**
How was my self -talk today? Circle One:	How was my focus today? Add up to 100% :	Did I commit to my plan? **Y/N**
POSITIVE	PAST: __%	Did I seek feedback?
NEUTRAL	**PRESENT: __%**	**Y/N**
NEGATIVE	FUTURE: __%	

WHAT I DID WELL:

_____

_____

_____

WHAT I LEARNED:

_____

_____

_____

WHAT I WILL WORK ON TO IMPROVE:

_____

_____

_____

OTHER THOUGHTS:

_____

_____

_____

THE MOST POWERFUL FORCE IS HOW YOU SEE YOURSELF

STRESS	**ENERGY**	**RECOVERY**
On a scale from 1-10	On a scale from 1-10	In the past 24 Hours
(1= low stress 10 = high stress)	(1= low energy 10 = high energy)	I slept for _____ hours
Circle One:	Circle One:	I napped for _____ min.
1 2 3	1 2 3	I practiced mindfulness
4 5 6 7	**4 5 6 7**	for _____ min.
8 9 10	**8 9 10**	

HOW DO I FEEL TODAY?

_____

_____

_____

GRATITUDE (I HAVE) — List recent small wins, things your experienced that made you happy, or what you are excited about.

_____

_____

_____

AFFIRMATIONS (I AM) — Give yourself positive self-talk. What actions have supported these affirmations?

_____

_____

_____

INTENTION (I WILL) — What is one area of your performance that you will focus on and/or try to execute?

_____

_____

BE PRESENT · BE AUTHENTIC · GROW DAILY

THOUGHTS	FOCUS	PROCESS
How was my self-talk today? Circle One: **POSITIVE NEUTRAL NEGATIVE**	How was my focus today? Add up to 100%: **PAST: __% PRESENT: __% FUTURE: __%**	Did I commit to my plan? **Y/N** Did I seek feedback? **Y/N**

WHAT I DID WELL:

_____
_____
_____

WHAT I LEARNED:

_____
_____
_____

WHAT I WILL WORK ON TO IMPROVE:

_____
_____
_____

OTHER THOUGHTS:

_____
_____
_____

3 WAYS TO BE A "G"
GENEROSITY - GRACE - GRATITUDE

STRESS	**ENERGY**	**RECOVERY**
On a scale from 1-10	On a scale from 1-10	In the past 24 Hours
(1= low stress 10 = high stress)	(1= low energy 10 = high energy)	
Circle One:	Circle One:	I slept for _____ hours
1 2 3	1 2 3	I napped for _____ min.
4 5 6 7	**4 5 6 7**	I practiced mindfulness
8 9 10	**8 9 10**	for _____ min.

HOW DO I FEEL TODAY?

_____

_____

_____

GRATITUDE (I HAVE) — List recent small wins, things your experienced that made you happy, or what you are excited about.

_____

_____

_____

AFFIRMATIONS (I AM) — Give yourself positive self-talk. What actions have supported these affirmations?

_____

_____

_____

INTENTION (I WILL) — What is one area of your performance that you will focus on and/or try to execute?

_____

_____

BE PRESENT • BE AUTHENTIC • GROW DAILY

THOUGHTS	FOCUS	PROCESS
How was my self -talk today? Circle One: POSITIVE **NEUTRAL** NEGATIVE	How was my focus today? Add up to 100% : PAST: __% **PRESENT: __%** FUTURE: __%	Did I commit to my plan? **Y/N** Did I seek feedback? **Y/N**

WHAT I DID WELL:

_____

_____

_____

WHAT I LEARNED:

_____

_____

_____

WHAT I WILL WORK ON TO IMPROVE:

_____

_____

_____

OTHER THOUGHTS:

_____

_____

_____

BE WHERE YOUR FEET ARE

STRESS	ENERGY	RECOVERY
On a scale from 1-10	On a scale from 1-10	In the past 24 Hours
(1= low stress 10 = high stress)	(1= low energy 10 = high energy)	
Circle One:	Circle One:	I slept for _____ hours
1 2 3	1 2 3	I napped for _____ min.
4 5 6 7	**4 5 6 7**	I practiced mindfulness
8 9 10	**8 9 10**	for _____ min.

HOW DO I FEEL TODAY?

_____

_____

_____

GRATITUDE (I HAVE) — List recent small wins, things your experienced that made you happy, or what you are excited about.

_____

_____

_____

AFFIRMATIONS (I AM) — Give yourself positive self-talk. What actions have supported these affirmations?

_____

_____

_____

INTENTION (I WILL) — What is one area of your performance that you will focus on and/or try to execute?

_____

_____

BE PRESENT · BE AUTHENTIC · GROW DAILY

THOUGHTS	FOCUS	PROCESS
How was my self -talk today? Circle One:	How was my focus today? Add up to 100% :	Did I commit to my plan?
POSITIVE	PAST: __%	Y / N
NEUTRAL	**PRESENT: __%**	Did I seek feedback?
NEGATIVE	FUTURE: __%	Y / N

WHAT I DID WELL:

_____
_____
_____

WHAT I LEARNED:

_____
_____
_____

WHAT I WILL WORK ON TO IMPROVE:

_____
_____
_____

OTHER THOUGHTS:

_____
_____
_____

DO THINGS WITH PURPOSE, ON PURPOSE

STRESS	**ENERGY**	**RECOVERY**
On a scale from 1-10	On a scale from 1-10	In the past 24 Hours
(1= low stress 10 = high stress)	(1= low energy 10 = high energy)	
Circle One:	Circle One:	I slept for _____ hours
1 2 3	1 2 3	I napped for _____ min.
4 5 6 7	**4 5 6 7**	I practiced mindfulness
8 9 10	**8 9 10**	for _____ min.

HOW DO I FEEL TODAY?

_____

_____

_____

GRATITUDE (I HAVE) — List recent small wins, things your experienced that made you happy, or what you are excited about.

_____

_____

_____

AFFIRMATIONS (I AM) — Give yourself positive self-talk. What actions have supported these affirmations?

_____

_____

_____

INTENTION (I WILL) — What is one area of your performance that you will focus on and/or try to execute?

_____

_____

BE PRESENT • BE AUTHENTIC • GROW DAILY

THOUGHTS	**FOCUS**	**PROCESS**
How was my self-talk today? Circle One:	How was my focus today? Add up to 100% :	Did I commit to my plan?
POSITIVE	PAST: __%	**Y/N**
NEUTRAL	**PRESENT: __%**	Did I seek feedback?
NEGATIVE	FUTURE: __%	**Y/N**

WHAT I DID WELL:

_____
_____
_____

WHAT I LEARNED:

_____
_____
_____

WHAT I WILL WORK ON TO IMPROVE:

_____
_____
_____

OTHER THOUGHTS:

_____
_____
_____

W.I.N. STANDS FOR:
WHAT'S IMPORTANT NOW

STRESS	**ENERGY**	**RECOVERY**
On a scale from 1-10	On a scale from 1-10	In the past 24 Hours
(1= low stress 10 = high stress)	(1= low energy 10 = high energy)	
Circle One:	Circle One:	I slept for _____ hours
1 2 3	1 2 3	I napped for _____ min.
4 5 6 7	**4 5 6 7**	I practiced mindfulness
8 9 10	**8 9 10**	for _____ min.

HOW DO I FEEL TODAY?

_____

_____

_____

GRATITUDE (I HAVE) — List recent small wins, things your experienced that made you happy, or what you are excited about.

_____

_____

_____

AFFIRMATIONS (I AM) — Give yourself positive self-talk. What actions have supported these affirmations?

_____

_____

_____

INTENTION (I WILL) — What is one area of your performance that you will focus on and/or try to execute?

_____

_____

BE PRESENT • BE AUTHENTIC • GROW DAILY

THOUGHTS	**FOCUS**	**PROCESS**
How was my self-talk today? Circle One:	How was my focus today? Add up to 100% :	Did I commit to my plan? **Y/N** Did I seek feedback? **Y/N**
POSITIVE **NEUTRAL** NEGATIVE	PAST: ___% PRESENT: __% FUTURE: ___%	

WHAT I DID WELL:

_____

_____

_____

WHAT I LEARNED:

_____

_____

_____

WHAT I WILL WORK ON TO IMPROVE:

_____

_____

_____

OTHER THOUGHTS:

_____

_____

_____

**DOES THE ROOM LIGHT UP
WHEN YOU ENTER OR WHEN YOU LEAVE?**

STRESS	**ENERGY**	**RECOVERY**
On a scale from 1-10	On a scale from 1-10	In the past 24 Hours
(1= low stress 10 = high stress)	(1= low energy 10 = high energy)	
Circle One:	Circle One:	I slept for _____ hours
1 2 3	1 2 3	I napped for _____ min.
4 5 6 7	**4 5 6 7**	I practiced mindfulness
8 9 10	**8 9 10**	for _____ min.

HOW DO I FEEL TODAY?

_____

_____

_____

GRATITUDE (I HAVE) — List recent small wins, things your experienced that made you happy, or what you are excited about.

_____

_____

_____

AFFIRMATIONS (I AM) — Give yourself positive self-talk. What actions have supported these affirmations?

_____

_____

_____

INTENTION (I WILL) — What is one area of your performance that you will focus on and/or try to execute?

_____

_____

BE PRESENT • BE AUTHENTIC • GROW DAILY

THOUGHTS	**FOCUS**	**PROCESS**
How was my self-talk today?	How was my focus today?	Did I commit to my plan?
Circle One:	Add up to 100% :	**Y / N**
POSITIVE	**PAST:** __%	Did I seek feedback?
NEUTRAL	**PRESENT:** __%	**Y / N**
NEGATIVE	**FUTURE:** __%	

WHAT I DID WELL:

_____

_____

_____

WHAT I LEARNED:

_____

_____

_____

WHAT I WILL WORK ON TO IMPROVE:

_____

_____

_____

OTHER THOUGHTS:

_____

_____

_____

THOUGHTS INFLUENCE HOW WE FEEL.
HOW WE FEEL INFLUENCES HOW WE PERFORM.

STRESS	**ENERGY**	**RECOVERY**
On a scale from 1-10	On a scale from 1-10	In the past 24 Hours
(1= low stress 10 = high stress)	(1= low energy 10 = high energy)	
Circle One:	Circle One:	I slept for _____ hours
1 2 3	1 2 3	I napped for _____ min.
4 5 6 7	**4 5 6 7**	I practiced mindfulness
8 9 10	**8 9 10**	for _____ min.

HOW DO I FEEL TODAY?

_____

_____

_____

GRATITUDE (I HAVE) — List recent small wins, things your experienced that made you happy, or what you are excited about.

_____

_____

_____

AFFIRMATIONS (I AM) — Give yourself positive self-talk. What actions have supported these affirmations?

_____

_____

_____

INTENTION (I WILL) — What is one area of your performance that you will focus on and/or try to execute?

_____

_____

BE PRESENT • BE AUTHENTIC • GROW DAILY

THOUGHTS	FOCUS	PROCESS
How was my self-talk today? Circle One:	How was my focus today? Add up to 100% :	Did I commit to my plan?
POSITIVE	PAST: ___%	**Y/N**
NEUTRAL	**PRESENT: __%**	Did I seek feedback?
NEGATIVE	FUTURE: ___%	**Y/N**

WHAT I DID WELL:

_____
_____
_____

WHAT I LEARNED:

_____
_____
_____

WHAT I WILL WORK ON TO IMPROVE:

_____
_____
_____

OTHER THOUGHTS:

_____
_____
_____

COURAGE COMES BEFORE CONFIDENCE

STRESS	**ENERGY**	**RECOVERY**
On a scale from 1-10	On a scale from 1-10	In the past 24 Hours
(1= low stress 10 = high stress)	(1= low energy 10 = high energy)	
Circle One:	Circle One:	I slept for _____ hours
1 2 3	1 2 3	I napped for _____ min.
4 5 6 7	**4 5 6 7**	I practiced mindfulness
8 9 10	**8 9 10**	for _____ min.

HOW DO I FEEL TODAY?

_____

_____

_____

GRATITUDE (I HAVE) — List recent small wins, things your experienced that made you happy, or what you are excited about.

_____

_____

_____

AFFIRMATIONS (I AM) — Give yourself positive self-talk. What actions have supported these affirmations?

_____

_____

_____

INTENTION (I WILL) — What is one area of your performance that you will focus on and/or try to execute?

_____

_____

BE PRESENT · BE AUTHENTIC · GROW DAILY

THOUGHTS	**FOCUS**	**PROCESS**
How was my self-talk today? Circle One:	How was my focus today? Add up to 100% :	Did I commit to my plan? **Y/N**
POSITIVE **NEUTRAL** **NEGATIVE**	**PAST: __%** **PRESENT: __%** **FUTURE: __%**	Did I seek feedback? **Y/N**

WHAT I DID WELL:

_____

_____

_____

WHAT I LEARNED:

_____

_____

_____

WHAT I WILL WORK ON TO IMPROVE:

_____

_____

_____

OTHER THOUGHTS:

_____

_____

_____

THERE ARE TWO PAINS IN LIFE: THE PAIN OF REGRET AND THE PAIN OF HARD WORK.

STRESS	**ENERGY**	**RECOVERY**
On a scale from 1-10	On a scale from 1-10	In the past 24 Hours
(1= low stress 10 = high stress)	(1= low energy 10 = high energy)	
Circle One:	Circle One:	I slept for _____ hours
1 2 3	1 2 3	I napped for _____ min.
4 5 6 7	**4 5 6 7**	I practiced mindfulness
8 9 10	**8 9 10**	for _____ min.

HOW DO I FEEL TODAY?

_____

_____

_____

GRATITUDE (I HAVE) — List recent small wins, things your experienced that made you happy, or what you are excited about.

_____

_____

_____

AFFIRMATIONS (I AM) — Give yourself positive self-talk. What actions have supported these affirmations?

_____

_____

_____

INTENTION (I WILL) — What is one area of your performance that you will focus on and/or try to execute?

_____

_____

BE PRESENT · BE AUTHENTIC · GROW DAILY

THOUGHTS	FOCUS	PROCESS
How was my self -talk today? Circle One: POSITIVE NEUTRAL NEGATIVE	How was my focus today? Add up to 100% : PAST: __% PRESENT: __% FUTURE: __%	Did I commit to my plan? Y/N Did I seek feedback? Y/N

WHAT I DID WELL:

_____

_____

_____

WHAT I LEARNED:

_____

_____

_____

WHAT I WILL WORK ON TO IMPROVE:

_____

_____

_____

OTHER THOUGHTS:

_____

_____

_____

FOCUS ON THE PROCESS NOT THE PRIZE

STRESS	**ENERGY**	**RECOVERY**
On a scale from 1-10	On a scale from 1-10	In the past 24 Hours
(1= low stress 10 = high stress)	(1= low energy 10 = high energy)	
Circle One:	Circle One:	I slept for _____ hours
1 2 3	1 2 3	I napped for _____ min.
4 5 6 7	**4 5 6 7**	I practiced mindfulness
8 9 10	**8 9 10**	for _____ min.

HOW DO I FEEL TODAY?

_____

_____

_____

GRATITUDE (I HAVE) — List recent small wins, things your experienced that made you happy, or what you are excited about.

_____

_____

_____

AFFIRMATIONS (I AM) — Give yourself positive self-talk. What actions have supported these affirmations?

_____

_____

_____

INTENTION (I WILL) — What is one area of your performance that you will focus on and/or try to execute?

_____

_____

BE PRESENT · BE AUTHENTIC · GROW DAILY

THOUGHTS	FOCUS	PROCESS
How was my self -talk today? Circle One:	How was my focus today? Add up to 100% :	Did I commit to my plan?
POSITIVE		**Y/N**
NEUTRAL	PAST: __%	Did I seek feedback?
NEGATIVE	PRESENT: __%	**Y/N**
	FUTURE: __%	

WHAT I DID WELL:

_____

_____

_____

WHAT I LEARNED:

_____

_____

_____

WHAT I WILL WORK ON TO IMPROVE:

_____

_____

_____

OTHER THOUGHTS:

WORRYING IS BETTING AGAINST YOURSELF

STRESS	ENERGY	RECOVERY
On a scale from 1-10 (1= low stress 10 = high stress) Circle One:	On a scale from 1-10 (1= low energy 10 = high energy) Circle One:	In the past 24 Hours
1 2 3 **4 5 6 7** 8 9 10	1 2 3 **4 5 6 7** **8 9 10**	I slept for _____ hours I napped for _____ min. I practiced mindfulness for _____ min.

HOW DO I FEEL TODAY?

_____

_____

_____

GRATITUDE (I HAVE) — List recent small wins, things your experienced that made you happy, or what you are excited about.

_____

_____

_____

AFFIRMATIONS (I AM) — Give yourself positive self-talk. What actions have supported these affirmations?

_____

_____

_____

INTENTION (I WILL) — What is one area of your performance that you will focus on and/or try to execute?

_____

_____

BE PRESENT · BE AUTHENTIC · GROW DAILY

THOUGHTS	**FOCUS**	**PROCESS**
How was my self-talk today? Circle One:	How was my focus today? Add up to 100% :	Did I commit to my plan?
		Y/N
POSITIVE	**PAST: __%**	Did I seek feedback?
NEUTRAL	**PRESENT: __%**	**Y/N**
NEGATIVE	**FUTURE: __%**	

WHAT I DID WELL:

_____

_____

_____

WHAT I LEARNED:

_____

_____

_____

WHAT I WILL WORK ON TO IMPROVE:

_____

_____

_____

OTHER THOUGHTS:

_____

_____

_____

WE RISE BY HELPING OTHERS

STRESS	ENERGY	RECOVERY
On a scale from 1-10 (1= low stress 10 = high stress) Circle One:	On a scale from 1-10 (1= low energy 10 = high energy) Circle One:	In the past 24 Hours
1 2 3 **4 5 6 7** 8 9 10	1 2 3 **4 5 6 7** **8 9 10**	I slept for _____ hours I napped for _____ min. I practiced mindfulness for _____ min.

HOW DO I FEEL TODAY?

_____

_____

_____

GRATITUDE (I HAVE) — List recent small wins, things your experienced that made you happy, or what you are excited about.

_____

_____

_____

AFFIRMATIONS (I AM) — Give yourself positive self-talk. What actions have supported these affirmations?

_____

_____

_____

INTENTION (I WILL) — What is one area of your performance that you will focus on and/or try to execute?

_____

_____

BE PRESENT • BE AUTHENTIC • GROW DAILY

THOUGHTS	**FOCUS**	**PROCESS**
How was my self -talk today? Circle One:	How was my focus today? Add up to 100% :	Did I commit to my plan? **Y/N**
POSITIVE **NEUTRAL** NEGATIVE	PAST: __% **PRESENT: __%** FUTURE: __%	Did I seek feedback? **Y/N**

WHAT I DID WELL:

_____

_____

_____

WHAT I LEARNED:

_____

_____

_____

WHAT I WILL WORK ON TO IMPROVE:

_____

_____

_____

OTHER THOUGHTS:

_____

_____

_____

YOU WERE DESIGNED FOR A REASON

STRESS	**ENERGY**	**RECOVERY**
On a scale from 1-10	On a scale from 1-10	In the past 24 Hours
(1= low stress 10 = high stress)	(1= low energy 10 = high energy)	I slept for _____ hours
Circle One:	Circle One:	
1 2 3	1 2 3	I napped for _____ min.
4 5 6 7	**4 5 6 7**	I practiced mindfulness
8 9 10	**8 9 10**	for _____ min.

HOW DO I FEEL TODAY?

_____

_____

_____

GRATITUDE (I HAVE) — List recent small wins, things your experienced that made you happy, or what you are excited about.

_____

_____

_____

AFFIRMATIONS (I AM) — Give yourself positive self-talk. What actions have supported these affirmations?

_____

_____

_____

INTENTION (I WILL) — What is one area of your performance that you will focus on and/or try to execute?

_____

_____

BE PRESENT • BE AUTHENTIC • GROW DAILY

THOUGHTS	**FOCUS**	**PROCESS**
How was my self -talk today? Circle One:	How was my focus today? Add up to 100% :	Did I commit to my plan?
POSITIVE	PAST: __%	**Y / N**
NEUTRAL	**PRESENT: __%**	Did I seek feedback?
NEGATIVE	FUTURE: __%	**Y / N**

WHAT I DID WELL:

_____

_____

_____

WHAT I LEARNED:

_____

_____

_____

WHAT I WILL WORK ON TO IMPROVE:

_____

_____

_____

OTHER THOUGHTS:

_____

_____

_____

CLUTCH MEANS DOING WHAT YOU NORMALLY CAN DO WHEN IT MATTERS MOST

STRESS	ENERGY	RECOVERY
On a scale from 1-10 (1= low stress 10 = high stress) Circle One:	On a scale from 1-10 (1= low energy 10 = high energy) Circle One:	In the past 24 Hours
1 2 3	1 2 3	I slept for _____ hours
4 5 6 7	**4 5 6 7**	I napped for _____ min.
8 9 10	**8 9 10**	I practiced mindfulness for _____ min.

HOW DO I FEEL TODAY?

_____

_____

_____

GRATITUDE (I HAVE) — List recent small wins, things your experienced that made you happy, or what you are excited about.

_____

_____

_____

AFFIRMATIONS (I AM) — Give yourself positive self-talk. What actions have supported these affirmations?

_____

_____

_____

INTENTION (I WILL) — What is one area of your performance that you will focus on and/or try to execute?

_____

_____

BE PRESENT • BE AUTHENTIC • GROW DAILY

THOUGHTS	FOCUS	PROCESS
How was my self -talk today? Circle One:	How was my focus today? Add up to 100% :	Did I commit to my plan?
POSITIVE		Y/N
NEUTRAL	PAST: __%	Did I seek feedback?
NEGATIVE	PRESENT: __% FUTURE: __%	Y/N

WHAT I DID WELL:

_____

_____

_____

WHAT I LEARNED:

_____

_____

_____

WHAT I WILL WORK ON TO IMPROVE:

_____

_____

_____

OTHER THOUGHTS:

_____

_____

_____

WE DON'T RISE TO THE OCCASION -
WE RISE TO OUR TRAINING

STRESS	**ENERGY**	**RECOVERY**
On a scale from 1-10 (1= low stress 10 = high stress) Circle One:	On a scale from 1-10 (1= low energy 10 = high energy) Circle One:	In the past 24 Hours
1 2 3	1 2 3	I slept for _____ hours
4 5 6 7	**4 5 6 7**	I napped for _____ min.
8 9 10	**8 9 10**	I practiced mindfulness for _____ min.

HOW DO I FEEL TODAY?

_____

_____

_____

GRATITUDE (I HAVE) — List recent small wins, things your experienced that made you happy, or what you are excited about.

_____

_____

_____

AFFIRMATIONS (I AM) — Give yourself positive self-talk. What actions have supported these affirmations?

_____

_____

_____

INTENTION (I WILL) — What is one area of your performance that you will focus on and/or try to execute?

_____

_____

BE PRESENT · BE AUTHENTIC · GROW DAILY

THOUGHTS	FOCUS	PROCESS
How was my self-talk today? Circle One:	How was my focus today? Add up to 100% :	Did I commit to my plan?
POSITIVE	**PAST: __%**	**Y/N**
NEUTRAL	**PRESENT: __%**	Did I seek feedback?
NEGATIVE	**FUTURE: __%**	**Y/N**

WHAT I DID WELL:

_____

_____

_____

WHAT I LEARNED:

_____

_____

_____

WHAT I WILL WORK ON TO IMPROVE:

_____

_____

_____

OTHER THOUGHTS:

_____

_____

_____

WHATEVER THE BRAIN CAN CONCEIVE AND BELIEVE, IT CAN ACHIEVE

STRESS	ENERGY	RECOVERY
On a scale from 1-10	On a scale from 1-10	In the past 24 Hours
(1= low stress 10 = high stress)	(1= low energy 10 = high energy)	
Circle One:	Circle One:	I slept for _____ hours
1 2 3	1 2 3	I napped for _____ min.
4 5 6 7	**4 5 6 7**	I practiced mindfulness
8 9 10	**8 9 10**	for _____ min.

HOW DO I FEEL TODAY?

_____

_____

_____

GRATITUDE (I HAVE) — List recent small wins, things your experienced that made you happy, or what you are excited about.

_____

_____

_____

AFFIRMATIONS (I AM) — Give yourself positive self-talk. What actions have supported these affirmations?

_____

_____

_____

INTENTION (I WILL) — What is one area of your performance that you will focus on and/or try to execute?

_____

_____

BE PRESENT · BE AUTHENTIC · GROW DAILY

THOUGHTS	FOCUS	PROCESS
How was my self-talk today? Circle One:	How was my focus today? Add up to 100% :	Did I commit to my plan?
POSITIVE	PAST: __%	**Y/N**
NEUTRAL	**PRESENT: __%**	Did I seek feedback?
NEGATIVE	FUTURE: __%	**Y/N**

WHAT I DID WELL:

_____

_____

_____

WHAT I LEARNED:

_____

_____

_____

WHAT I WILL WORK ON TO IMPROVE:

_____

_____

_____

OTHER THOUGHTS:

_____

_____

_____

NO ONE SHOULD WIN OR WORRY ALONE

STRESS	**ENERGY**	**RECOVERY**
On a scale from 1-10 (1= low stress 10 = high stress) Circle One: **1 2 3** **4 5 6 7** 8 9 10	On a scale from 1-10 (1= low energy 10 = high energy) Circle One: 1 2 3 **4 5 6 7** **8 9 10**	In the past 24 Hours I slept for _____ hours I napped for _____ min. I practiced mindfulness for _____ min.

HOW DO I FEEL TODAY?

_____

_____

_____

GRATITUDE (I HAVE) — List recent small wins, things your experienced that made you happy, or what you are excited about.

_____

_____

_____

AFFIRMATIONS (I AM) — Give yourself positive self-talk. What actions have supported these affirmations?

_____

_____

_____

INTENTION (I WILL) — What is one area of your performance that you will focus on and/or try to execute?

_____

_____

_____

BE PRESENT • BE AUTHENTIC • GROW DAILY

THOUGHTS
How was my
self -talk today?
Circle One:

POSITIVE
NEUTRAL
NEGATIVE

FOCUS
How was my focus today?
Add up to 100% :

PAST: __%
PRESENT: __%
FUTURE: __%

PROCESS
Did I commit to my plan?

Y/N

Did I seek feedback?

Y/N

WHAT I DID WELL:

WHAT I LEARNED:

WHAT I WILL WORK ON TO IMPROVE:

OTHER THOUGHTS:

GO THE EXTRA MILE - IT'S NEVER CROWDED

NOTES

Made in the USA
San Bernardino, CA
04 May 2019